INDIANS OF SOUTHERN ILLINOIS

INDIANS OF
SOUTHERN ILLINOIS

By

IRVIN M. PEITHMANN

Department of Recreation and Outdoor Education
Southern Illinois University
Carbondale, Illinois

CHARLES C THOMAS • PUBLISHER
Springfield • Illinois • U.S.A.

Published and Distributed Throughout the World by

CHARLES C THOMAS • PUBLISHER

BANNERSTONE HOUSE

301-327 East Lawrence Avenue, Springfield, Illinois, U.S.A.

NATCHEZ PLANTATION HOUSE

735 North Atlantic Boulevard, Fort Lauderdale, Florida, U.S.A.

With THOMAS BOOKS careful attention is given to all details of manufacturing and design. It is the Publisher's desire to present books that are satisfactory as to their physical qualities and artistic possibilities and appropriate for their particular use. THOMAS BOOKS will be true to those laws of quality that assure a good name and good will

Printed in the United States of America

G-2

To My Father and Mother

My Best Friends

Introduction

I HAVE WRITTEN this book for those who wish to know something of the archaeology and prehistory of the Indians who lived in southern Illinois. I grew up in this country of which I write. As a boy, I rambled over Indian camp sites along the Kaskaskia River. Love of the out-of-doors asserted itself, and at every opportunity I took to the country lanes and roads in search of some unexplored Indian camp site. I often thought of the people who had lived at these sites and wondered what they looked like, how long ago they lived, and how they used many of the things I found.

As long as I remember, my thoughts have been interwoven with stories of Indians. My father, who had lived in Indian Territory (now Oklahoma) over sixty years ago, often spoke of the Indians and how they lived in the Territory.

The "old-timers," who knew nothing of the real story of the Indians living here before the coming of the white men, told me many fictitious and imaginative stories of prehistoric Indians. I did not know then that the "arrowheads" I found and treasured were really flint knives, lances or spearheads used on shafts by a hunting people who did not know of the bow. Nor did I know that the small triangular flint points called "warpoints" were arrowheads left by a later people who did use the bow and arrow in hunting. On some Indian camp sites I found no pottery fragments, but, instead, I found flint spearheads, knife blades and, occasionally, grooved stone axes. I learned many years later that the prehistoric Indians of the Archaic period had lived at these places. Other Indian sites had flint tools and pottery fragments of different styles. As a boy, I did not know that these sites were former living places of Woodland, Hopewell, and Mississippi Indians.

When I left my rural home near Hoyleton, Illinois, and moved to Carbondale, where I was employed as farm manager on the university farm, I continued my interest in Indian history. I read available books on archaeology but found that little had been written about the Indians of southern Illinois. Some years later, when I was transferred to the university museum, I continued to read books on archaeology. I came in contact with professional archaeologists and learned much from them. Summers were spent in the field with representatives of other museums and universities excavating sites I had previously reported to them. I added photography to my hobbies and started keeping photographic records of findings made during excavations and field reconnaissance.

This book, which stems from boyhood findings, such as arrowheads, warpoints, and pottery fragments, is the result of many happy days of comradeship, camping and tramping, photographing, and research along the rivers and streams and over the hills of southern Illinois. It is part of the story of how people lived through the centuries and vanished long ago into the mists of history. We are white men, but the red men lived here first and left behind many things to remind us of their history, traditions and cultures. One who thinks of the former inhabitants of southern Illinois only as "Indians" has missed something of the traditions of the past as well as values for the present.

Through the years, man everywhere in the world has looked for security, which has not been possible, for he is a part of nature and must face the hazards of nature, fight them with individual courage and try to conquer them alone.

The Indian who lived here for many centuries learned that, in order to survive, he had to meet the challenge in unfriendly surroundings and that he too was sometimes confronted with starvation and inadequate shelter for his family, due to forced migration caused by a lack of available food or by enemies who had driven him out. How the prehistoric red men solved or failed to solve these problems is of great importance in helping us understand this aspect of the American past. The archaeology and history of southern Illinois are truly a part of our heritage.

In gathering material for this book the author traveled widely over the United States for the past seven years, visiting numerous Indian reservations in the West. In 1951-52, he made several trips to Oklahoma, where he studied the Indians living in this area. In 1953, as assistant director on a southern Illinois geography field tour of Canada, Alaska and our Northwest, he observed the Indians living in these regions. His former position as Curator of Archaeology of the Southern Illinois University Museum has also been of great service in his research for this book.

As one reads a road map and follows the highways of southern Illinois, the names of rivers and towns bring back memories of Indian tribes, chiefs and settlements. The word "Illinois" is of Indian origin. The Illinois Confederacy was a group of historic tribes belonging to the Algonquin linguistic stock, consisting of six tribes—the Cahokias, the Kaskaskia, the Michigamea, the Moingwena, the Peoria, and the Tamaroa—who called themselves Inini—later Illini ("superior or real men"). Several of these tribes came to southern Illinois to live.[1]

Our region is bounded on the east by the Wabash and Ohio rivers and by the Mississippi River on the west. As one enters the region from any direction, one is likely to cross rivers and drive through towns with Indian names: Cahokia, Nokomis, Okawville, Mascoutah, Tamaroa, Shawneetown, and Kaskaskia.

Today many people are still seeking information as to how these Indians lived. Scientists attempt to collect information just as a detective gathers information to solve a crime. These scientists, who are called archaeologists, are at work today. They try to interpret the evidence they find and "make the past live again." As they collect new evidence, we sometimes have to discard our old ideas of how the prehistoric Indians lived.

We have failed to recognize the work of some of the early archaeologists and students of archaeology partly because their methods were not up to present-day standards. In spite of this fact, their contributions were many. Sometimes we still hear criticism made of the lay or amateur archaeologists; however, they have made many of the important finds for the professional archaeologists to interpret.

---

[1]See p. 104

In southern Illinois if one looks and listens, he will learn something of the archaeologists' interpretation of these findings, and he will recognize a kinship with the red man and an indebtedness to him.

Acknowledgments

THE AUTHOR wishes to acknowledge his indebtedness for the helpful suggestions and criticisms received from many sources in compiling the data for this book.

The author is especially grateful to Dr. Thomas F. Barton, of the Geography Department of Indiana University; to Dr. Thorne Deuel, Director of the Illinois State Museum; to Mr. Glenn A. Black, Angel Mounds, Newburgh, Indiana; and to Mr. John Allen, of Southern Illinois University, all of whom gave valuable assistance that helped make this volume possible. Thanks are also due to the many other faculty members of Southern Illinois University for their interest and suggestions.

Grateful acknowledgements are made to the Southern Illinois University Photographic Service, to the Illinois State Museum and to Grover Brinkman and Solon Bartnek for their kind permission to reprint some of the photographs in this book.

The author wishes also to acknowledge his debt to his wife and his sons, Russell and Albert, who share his interest in archaeology and, particularly, to Russell for those of his drawings that have been used in this book.

I. M. P.

Contents

xiii

INDIANS OF SOUTHERN ILLINOIS

Part One

The Region

WEDGED IN BY two great rivers, the Ohio on the east and Mississippi on the west, there is a region called southern Illinois. Within this geographic boundary lies one of the most attractive areas in the Midwest from an archaeological and historical standpoint. Southern Illinois is often called "Egypt," partly because of its fancied resemblance to the Delta of the Nile, and partly because of the modern city of Cairo, which is situated at the confluence of these two great rivers.

The Mississippi and Ohio rivers came into existence for the most part during the past million years, a period geologists refer to as the Pleistocene. Great sheets of ice that lay over eastern Canada and northeastern United States began to melt and send floodwaters on their way to the Gulf of Mexico, working out deep valleys. Long ranges of limestone and sandstone bluffs were carved out by the action of the glacial waters where the Ozark hill range crosses these rivers. The results of this action are most noticeable near Grand Tower, at Fountain Bluff, and southeastward along the east side of the river flood plain.

The glacier that during this age covered most of Illinois to a point south of Carbondale is known to geologists as the Illinoisan. Evidence of this glacier is shown in exposed places in creek and river banks by characteristic pebblestones of greenstone, granite, and other rocks brought down from the north by this glacier. A warm period caused it to melt; the area became very dry. The prevailing westerly winds during this period swept across dry barren lands, creating great dust storms, and deposited wind-blown soil called loess to a depth of many feet on top of the glacial deposits. This wind-blown silt can still be seen in many places where it was scattered by the winds and piled up, creating the hills and bluffs along the east side of the Mississippi

River flood plain. It is most noticeable along the river bluffs east of East St. Louis and southward along the river. All of this took place centuries before the first prehistoric Indians came to live in southern Illinois.

Some botanists now believe that during this earlier time the whole area was a vast grassland, the forests making their appearance at at much later date. The first encroachment of the forests was along the large rivers and streams.

A. French Explorers' Description of the Area

Even as late as the latter part of the seventeenth century, the forests observed by the first explorers were sparse compared to the later densely timbered tracts, some of which have not been destroyed and have remained until today. Early travelers and explorers reported that most of the hill country was either in prairie-like grassland or parklike timber, with the trees widely dispersed.

Botanists have not based their conclusions entirely on the observations of these early reports, but on the geological and ecological aspects of the area. Several factors apparently caused the tree invasion which has, within the past one hundred and fifty years, covered the area with heavier and denser forests. The Indians had for centuries set fire to the grassland during the fall hunting season (Indian summer). They used this method to drive and stampede such game as elk, deer, and later, probably, bison. As the land was settled, fires, which were a threat to the white man's clearings, became fewer; though there were fires, they were limited in scope and kept under some control. My father told me that his grandmother often spoke of the timber and prairie fires that periodically swept over the area (which is now Washington County) where she lived over one hundred years ago. As these fires which served to keep out the tree invasion ended, the trees came crowding in. There is also evidence that rainfall has become steadily heavier over the past centuries, which has enabled trees to invade the territory of the drought-resistant grasses.

B. Topography and Wildlife

Let us take a look at a map of southern Illinois for a moment and draw an imaginary line across the state from East St. Louis, on the Mississippi, eastward to Vincennes, on the Wabash. The topography of the land is gently rolling to rolling and the landscape is covered with a patchwork of timbered tracts and farmland.

Draw another line from Vandalia southward to Carbondale and there is no striking difference on the surface contour. South of Carbondale, near Makanda, an extension of the Ozark range crosses the area in a west-east direction. The highest points of the hills and ridges of this "rock-ribbed" range are interspersed with numerous gaps or valleys, which elk, deer, bison, Indians and, finally, white men used to traverse the area.

1. Vast Swampland

Lying south of this range of hills, between the two great rivers, there was a vast swampland covering many thousands of acres. When white men first saw it, they called it the "Big Swamp." In this primitive wilderness of cypress trees, water, and swampland, where the Cache River now meanders, the Indian hunters for many centuries paddled their dugouts in search of game and fish. A large part of this area has now been drained. Almost all of the large, bald cypress have been chopped down; only a few are left around Horseshoe Lake and other lakes (formerly old river channels) to remind us of a vanished primeval wilderness that once existed in this southern-most part of Illinois.

2. Animal Life

When white men first came to southern Illinois, they found an abundance of wild game such as bison, elk, deer, bear, panther, wolf, fox, beaver, otter, raccoon, mink, muskrat, opossum, wildcat, woodchuck, skunk, and squirrel. These animals had been hunted for centuries by the Indians for food and clothing.

The wild turkey, passenger pigeon, prairie chicken, and quail lived in the upland and timbered areas. There was then, as there is today, seasonal migration of geese and ducks along the Mississippi flyway. The large swan lived on or near the marshy lakes; a small parrot-like bird called the Carolina parakeet lived in the forests. Birds of prey, such as the hawk, osprey and bald eagle, built their nests on the rocky ledges and in the tops of large trees. The rivers and streams contained many varieties of fish. Southern Illinois was "good Indian country."

3. Rivers

The rivers that border southern Illinois were contributing factors that attracted the prehistoric Indians, through the centuries, to come and live in this area. They followed these rivers; however, this does not necessarily mean they all came in dugout boats.

The presence of the rivers and their tributaries in this area meant that there was ample vegetation near these waterways. Where there is vegetation, there is animal life—the subsistence for all hunting as well as semi-agricultural Indian groups.

These rivers bordering and crossing the region, which were so important to Indian travel for many centuries, were just as important to the first white men who came to explore. The French explorer Marquette probably was the first white man to see what is now southern Illinois during his explorations of the Mississippi River in the year 1673. Historical records tell us that he stopped at the mouth of Marys River near Chester (Randolph County) to visit with a tribe of Indians living there at the time.

Later the French trappers came to trade with the Indians, plying their wooden pirogues up and down the rivers and streams in search of fur-bearing animals and leaving marks of their culture behind them. Beaucoup Creek got its name from the French word, *beaucoup,* which means "much" or "many." The Mississippi River soon became the avenue for trade and commerce between the French towns in this area and New Orleans, the nearest seaport. Later, the Ohio River became the "highway" of the early settlers coming into southern Illinois after the Revolutionary War.

For more than a hundred and fifty years after the coming of white men, travel to and from a southern Illinois town was done on the waterways. Up to this time roads over the area were hardly more than trails, and railroads were still unheard of. Steamboats came into use during the first quarter of the nineteenth century, and their use continued into the twentieth century.

Today the area is crisscrossed by modern highways and railroads that connect each city and town; airports furnish rapid transportation to any part of the world in a few days; and what once were vast areas of forest and prairie are now modern farming communities.

Part Two

Cultures

A. Southern Illinois Indian Cultures

WHO WERE THE FIRST PEOPLE to inhabit the valleys, hills, and plains in this area of southern Illinois? How long ago did they inhabit this area? Where did they come from? Where and how did they live? Why did they vanish? These questions and many more come to mind when a person gives a little thought to the form of human life which existed here before records of history began. Although there will always be more questions than answers, we have more answers now than we had twenty-five years ago, and answers are always being discovered as scientific research progresses.

Several theories have been advanced to explain the presence of people in prehistoric America. One is that small groups of primitive people crossed the wide stretches of the Pacific Ocean on a raft or boat. However, archaeologists believe this to have been improbable. Another theory suggests that a hunting people in search of game came over from Asia across the Bering Strait, using a crude raft for the seventy-mile voyage or walking on a "land bridge" which is now under water. The latter idea, which is most widely accepted, holds the key to beliefs about the length of time people have lived in the Western Hemisphere.

The last Ice Age ended somewhere between 10,000 and 20,000 years ago. Most archaeologists have maintained that the first immigrants crossed the land bridge from Siberia to Alaska. Because sea water was concentrated in the sheet of ice which extended south into Illinois, the sea level was lower than it is now, and the crossing could have been made on dry land. According to this theory, the North and South American continents were sealed off from outside influences by the rising of the oceans, caused by the melting of the glacial ice cap, eliminating the land bridge

11

that had previously existed. Many achaeologists now believe that the Indians lived in complete isolation for thousands of years, many cultures later developing from these first people who found their way across the Bering Strait.

From the time of the earliest inhabitants, aboriginal hunting cultures developed and often lasted through the centuries, shaped mainly by the unrestrained forces of nature. As the years passed, so passed the hunters and their way of life. Succeeding cultures, with many variations, followed each other down through the years; in southern Illinois they were the Archaic, the Woodland, the Hopewellian, the Mississippian, and the historic Indians' culture. The American Indian is a member of the Mongoloid division of mankind. This does not mean that he is descended from the Chinese, but it does indicate a common ancestry with them. The fact that the Indians are Mongoloids further justifies that belief that they came by the easiest route from Asia.

In the past, when the subject of archaeology has been mentioned, most of us have thought of faraway lands where civilizations flourished and died many hundreds of years ago. We have not advertised and have overlooked and in other ways neglected the archaeology in our own back yard—in our own region of southern Illinois. Yet the Mississippi, the Ohio, the Wabash, the Kaskaskia, the Saline, and the Big Muddy rivers and their tributaries were major pathways of early Indian migrations in the centuries past. Here was the ancestral home of many Indians. The prints of their moccasins have long disappeared, but much evidence remains to remind us of an era when they held undisputed control over the hills and valleys of southern Illinois. Today, archaeologists find evidence of their former living places along these waterways. Here in this region, buried beneath the soil, many archaeological finds await discovery. Modern archaeology can reconstruct much of the everyday life from things found where the Indians lived. Once their village sites, workshops, flint quarries, and burial grounds are found, evidence of how they lived can be uncovered. We can reconstruct their way of living, what they ate, and the tools with which they hunted.

If an archaeologist could turn back the clock and would come to one of their villages, he would know beforehand what he would be served for dinner if invited to stay; their clothing and the tools and implements around their lodges would be familiar objects to him.

The quantity and type of evidence prove that thousands of people lived here at different periods; as one culture disappeared, another took its place. These successions of cultures have passed across the stage of time since the first aborigines came across the Bering Strait many thousands of years ago.

The idea that an Indian is an Indian is a viewpoint often taken, without taking into consideration that there were different groups, different languages, and cultures. Here, as elsewhere, archaeological study reveals man's struggle with himself and with the society in which he lived. It also reveals an insight into our present problems and those we face in the future. Problems such as a shifting or moving-about of aboriginal Indian populations and what happens when one group of people is forced to mingle with another may offer clues to present-day tensions now on a global scale brought about in the same general way.

Archaeologically speaking, a culture is a way of life—a way people live during a given period of time. A group of individuals in comparative isolation from other people develop habits and customs such as ways of hunting, building houses, farming, decorating their bodies. Soon they possess a series of traits with striking features that distinguish them from other groups. A culture, then, is a distinct way of domestic living. Cultures, or ways of life, have disappeared from time to time. This does not necessarily mean that the people completely vanished. Generally, through warfare or, possibly, epidemics, the stronger invaders overtook the weaker cultures, which lost their cultural identity. When two cultures clash, several things may happen. One culture may disappear, some of the traits of each may be continued, or an entirely new culture may develop from the intermingling of the two. Generally, there is an evolution with the interchanging or intermingling of two cultures, resulting in a new and superior culture.[1] Here in this area Indians built their communities, lived out their lives and disappeared. Down through the centuries

---

[1] See "Hopewellian Culture," p. 27.

a variety of different groups came and went. Cultures and customs often overlapped. Since each succeeding culture is related to its past, it is possible to start with the oldest and trace them forward in time. In a similar way one can trace the evolution of automobiles forward from the horseless buggy to our modern car, or backward from our modern car to the horseless buggy. Such a study gives us a general idea of prehistoric happenings and a better understanding of these early cultures.

In the following chapters an attempt will be made to describe these vanished cultures and to tell something of the people who formed them. We will start with the oldest; however, before presenting each of the distinct cultures which existed here in southern Illinois, it seems wise to digress and explain three terms which often confuse the lay archaeologist.

One of the first questions the layman is likely to ask is, "What is archaeology?" In order to have a clear understanding of archaeology, one must also know something of anthropology and ethnology. Anthropology is the study of man—his origin and development, embracing both the present and the past. Ethnology is different from archaeology only in point of time. It is a cultural study of historically existing society, or of people still living, based on facts obtained by actual observations of human customs in operation and on information gleaned from records left by early travelers and explorers of the historic period. Archaeology may be generally defined as a scientific study of any prehistoric culture which involves excavation and description of remains of formerly existing people. It is based, in part, upon material evidence (artifacts) obtained at sites of former occupation.

For example, from the archaeological study of the tools and implements of the Archaic and the early Woodland people we know they were hunters and fishermen and practiced little or no agriculture. These bands or groups depended on the food nature provided them in season, such as wild fruits, berries, and nuts, as well as on such wild animals, fish, and birds as they could catch. When these resources failed them, they could migrate to a more favorable place in order to sustain their simple way of life. By following the game about the area, they were assured of an available food supply.

In contrast, we know the culture of the Mississippi people five hundred years ago was that of a farming people living in permanent villages and towns in the river valleys; constructing temples and chiefs' houses on mounds; growing corn, beans, and squash; manufacturing pottery on a large scale; and manufacturing flint implements, such as hoes, to be used in the cultivation of crops.

Artifacts or relics—that is, things made by man such as flint implements, pipes, beads, pottery, and many other items used in their everyday life—give us some clear and detailed ideas of the culture or way of life of a vanished people. However, they do not tell the whole story. If you found one flint hoe on a village site, it would not tell you much; but if you found a hundred, or knew that many had been found there, then you would know at once that the people who once lived there had been an agricultural people.

In making a study of cultures there are certain traits or features involved that must be recognized. The tools, weapons, and implements used by a group imply a cultural trait; when you have a sample of all the tools, you have a cultural complex.

The handing down of beliefs and customs from ancestors was done by means of speech rather than by written records. Family traditions which were handed down from father to son and from mother to daughter offered only one way of life, since these families did not have a chance to study different people and to choose their way of life as we do today.

Physical environment has much to do with the culture of a people. For many centuries southern Illinois had an abundance of raw materials for food, shelter, tools, implements, and clothing, which all Indians used to their advantage. The archaeologists prove this for us by showing that the area was rich enough to support, at different times, people who left thousands of camping, living, and burial sites found here.

Of course, there were also times of drought and other times when food was scarce, and the Indians depending on a hunting and gathering economy had to migrate or starve. The Archaic and the Woodland Indians took nature about as they found it and sometimes became victimized by their own environment and had to move to change their circumstances, whereas the later, more advanced Mississippi Indians, and still later the white men, improved on the resources of nature.

Environment exerts a powerful influence on the life of any people; even today environment limits possibilities regardless of technology. The introduction of cultivated crops, such as maize (corn) and vegetables, to supplement the food supply changed the cultural environment. By doing this, a hunting people could live or continue to live in an area long after the supply of game became scarce.

The western plains Indians, as late as one hundred years ago, had depended on the herds of bison in order to find food. However, the Mississippi Indians who lived here for several centuries late in prehistoric times had advanced far enough to live in villages, build homes, erect temple mounds, and to develop a social and political organization of high order, all because they had learned to plant their own food and cultivate it. By overcoming some of the handicaps of natural environment, these people developed an advanced culture that distinguishes them from all others. As people advance in technology, they can use an environment in different and more useful ways.

Everything we have and use in our present civilization came about from simple beginnings. Bits of scientific and technical knowledge were the result of inventions and ideas over many hundreds and thousands of years. Our buildings, railroads, modern mechanical machinery, the sciences of chemistry and physics, and other knowledge are the results of ideas, experiments, inventions that have been continually improved upon for many centuries.

When white men came to live in America, they brought with them the ingenuity and technical knowledge developed up to that time. Because of these benefits they had one "strike" on the Indians from the beginning. The Indians could not read or write but had to depend on their memories. Ideas and ways of doing things were handed down from one generation to the next, and for this reason no records, formulas, or ways of doing things could be kept for future reference. Too, the Indians were isolated from inventions that were taking place in Europe and Asia.

The flint spearhead was an invention that the first hunting people brought with them to America. They learned to make pottery and take up farming only after living here for thousands of years. They lacked the technical knowledge and ways, sometimes, to improve the simplest inventions, such as the tools and implements they used. In different parts of this country they found iron and copper ore deposits, from which they mined the ores, but they lacked the knowledge necessary to utilize these ores to their fullest extent. They mined the ores and by grinding and shaping them made them into crude axes and other tools. They had the raw material to work with but lacked the "knowhow" to heat, smelt, refine, forge, and cast it into tools and mechanical devices that work for man. This is probably one of the reasons why the Indians who lived here for thousands of years did not progress from a series of aboriginal cultures to a civilization.

1. Early Hunters—Paleo-Indians

Columbus was looking for a shorter route to India when he discovered America. As a result, the people he found inhabiting the islands in the West Indies he called Indians. Archaeologists call all prehistoric people who lived in America Indians, though they lived here thousands of years before the discovery.

The ancestors of the earliest people who lived in southern Illinois came from Eurasia, just as our ancestors did. Our ancestors came west from Europe and migrated into southern Illinois from the eastern part of the United States and from the Atlantic coast and the Gulf of Mexico. The story of this migration is the written history of the United States. How the ancestors of the early hunting people who first lived in southern Illinois migrated east from Asia and then east across North America is a story which has been neglected. To consider it we must go back to geological times.

Geologists have found that during the time that the great ice sheet lay over much of Canada and our northeastern states, there was often grassland in Alaska. This grassland extended southeastward to the Gulf of Mexico and formed an ice-free

---

*The author traveled over the Alaska Highway during the summer of 1953 and observed the route presumably taken by these first Americans.

passage down the McKenzie Valley and along what is now the Alaska Highway.[2] This corridor existed, possibly, as long as twenty-five thousand years ago, at a time when it is thought by some that the Bering Strait was a land bridge. Near Fairbanks, Alaska, there have recently been found chipped flint spear points and cutting tools of the same pattern used by a hunting people who lived on the Gobi Desert in Siberia. Since the great ice sheets were a barrier on the east and the Rocky Mountains blocked the passage on the west, these early hunters migrated southward down the McKenzie Valley into Canada. Slowly at first, band after band moved in, and, finding good hunting, they moved southward through the forests to the lush grasslands of our western United States. Here, thousands of years later, archaeologists found clues that told of the movements of these first Americans.

After the last glacial period, ten thousand to twenty thousand years ago, there was a time when the area was wet and cool. Animals such as the mammoth, mastadon and giant bison which had been browsing around the Mississippi and Ohio valleys at that time, probably, began to die out. It is probable that the last of these huge animals had died before the first prehistoric man entered southern Illinois.

Sometime after this cold period drastic climatic changes were taking place and for a period of many centuries it became warm and dry. The scarcity of the game from which the early hunters derived their living probably forced them to migrate eastward, following the Missouri River into the Mississippi Valley. The chances of survival during this dry period were greater near the great waterways where vegetation and animal life existed.

The term "Paleo-Indian" (from the Greek word *paleo*— "old") refers to ancient nomadic Indian hunting groups who came from Asia at the end of the Ice Age about twenty thousand years ago. In recent years the earliest date which man is known to have existed in America has been moved back from ten thousand years ago to about twenty thousand years ago. During these early times different Indian groups lived and hunted in the western and southwestern United States. They made flint spear points archaeologists now call Sandia, Yuma, Clovis, and Folsom.

Probably the best-known archaeological evidences, proving

that Indians lived in America as early as twenty thousand years ago, were the discoveries made first in 1926 at Folsom, New Mexico, later at Fort Collins, Colorado, and at Clovis, New Mexico. These important finds have come to be known as the Folsom complex, characterized by a number of skillfully made fluted spear points with fossilized bones of mammoth, musk ox, wild horse and bison that lived during the glacial period. No human remains were found at any of these places.

A recent discovery near Midland, Texas, of a human skull and other bone fragments in association with the bones of a wild horse may furnish a clue as to the physical characteristics of these early Americans. The finding of Midland man may soon give us some idea of what these early hunters looked like. Midland man, according to fluorine tests and geological evidence, may have lived several thousand years before Folsom man.

The cultural history of North America begins with these first hunters. The fluted dart points called Folsom Fluted[3] have been found with the remains of extinct animals, such as the bison and the wild horse, showing us that man had lived at the same time as these animals, and that he had hunted them for food and clothing. The remains of mammoths and other extinct animals found so far in southern Illinois have produced no evidence that they were hunted by these early people. No hunting tools have been found associated with skeletons of these animals to indicate they had been killed by man.

Though no flint wood-working tools have been found to suggest that these Indians made dugout boats, the Mississippi River or any other river would not have been a barrier to these shrewd hunters, who were self-sufficient and wise in the ways and

---

[3]The flutes or grooves on the flat sides of fluted points have been called "blood grooves." The presence of grooves on the sides of these flint points has been thought by some people to have been made for the purpose of causing the animal being hunted to bleed more easily after being hit by one of these fluted points mounted on the end of a wooden shaft. The animal, after being struck during the chase, would then become weakened to the extent that the hunter could close in for the kill.

The best possible explanation for the presence of grooves on the sides of these points is that the grooves were made to fit each side of the wood shaft, which was then fastened with a gut string or other thread or cord made of sinew.

laws of nature. They left no traces of pottery or domesticated plants. Living by hunting alone, they probably carried all their possessions on their backs. Their hunting and cutting tools were of chipped flint. Fluted projectile points which have been found in southern Illinois in considerable numbers resemble somewhat the classic Folsom dart points found in New Mexico and Colorado among the remains of animals now extinct. For archaeology, the year 1926 was a turning point; it was at this time that the Folsom culture in the western United States was recognized as a distinct culture. The Indian hunters who lost the fluted points in southern Illinois were possible descendants of those early western hunters and had migrated into the Mississippi and Ohio valleys preceding the early Archaic period.

This, then, is a picture of what took place in the old Stone Age of aboriginal America. Here is the clue to who left the fluted points we find in southern Illinois and elsewhere in the Mississippi and Ohio valleys.

2. Archaic Period

Early Archaic

This age, probably over ten thousand years ago,[4] when these Indians first moved into the middle and eastern United States, is called the early Archaic period. Because of a dry period that probably lasted many centuries, climatic conditions were unfavorable for an abundant game supply. Therefore, only a limited number of people could reside in one place for a time. They were more or less wanderers, without permanent homes, hunting what game was available, gathering berries, grass seeds, roots, and nuts, and grinding them on milling-stones (mortars) for food.

---

[4] The oldest dated Indian site east of the Mississippi River is in southern Illinois.

Tests of carbon samples taken recently from Modoc rock shelter, in the Mississippi River bluffs near Prairie du Rocher in Randolph County, showed the date to be nearly eleven thousand years ago, when the site was first inhabited. Originally, archaeologists had placed a date of about seven thousand years as the earliest occupation at this rock shelter.

The tests were made from charcoal samples taken from a fire hearth twenty-six feet below the present surface or dirt floor of this shelter. This is the deepest archaeological excavation ever made in Illinois.

The author reported this site to the Illinois State Museum; excavations were started in 1952 and continued in 1953.

They way of life during this period was rather primitive, since they never advanced past a hunting and gathering economy —they made no pottery and knew little or no agriculture. They were people with a simple standard of living; it was always a battle to survive. In their aboriginal existence it was the survival of the fittest.

After this early period the migrations from Asia continued, diffusing new peoples and cultures over North America. Some of these people found their way into southern Illinois. During the Archaic period they had no pottery to cook in. The meat of the animals they hunted was either eaten raw or roasted over an open campfire.

The only animal they domesticated was the dog, which was used in good times as a helper and companion but in lean times as a source of food.

Late Archaic

Following this long dry period there came another climatic change which returned North America to a cool, wet climate. Animals and plant life which flourished under these ideal conditions were sufficient, therefore, to support the additional groups of people who were finding their way into the Mississippi and Ohio valleys.

During the late Archaic, possibly four or five thousand years ago, the hunting and living habits seem to have changed a little from those of the early Archaic period.

The location of many Archaic sites on high ground or ridges near streams and old lakes in the Cache River area suggests that some of their travel was done in dugout boats. Many of these sites, due to their size, suggest a rather permanent living place, while many of the smaller sites were more or less "stations" used from time to time while on hunting and fishing expeditions in the area and only inhabited for short periods of time. The Faulkner site in Massac County was an Archaic site which has been partly excavated and studied. It is only one of numerous Archaic sites in southern Illinois.

The type of stone hunting tools and weapons of these early hunting people, found at these sites, suggests the use of the spear or lance, the atlatl (spear-launcher), and the bola. They had not yet learned to use the bow and arrow. Because the Indians at the beginning of the historic period were using the spear or lance and the bow and arrow for hunting and warfare when they were first contacted by the explorers, it has been generally supposed that these tools and weapons had been used also by the prehistoric Indians for many centuries, but this was not the case. In terms of time period, the use of the bow and arrow is of comparatively recent origin and came into practice probably about the time when the prehistoric Mississippi people were coming to live in the Mississippi and Ohio valleys, probably about fifteen hundred years ago. The spear or lance probably was the one weapon that was used in prehistoric times and continued up to and into the historic period. Contrary to opinion, the long spear or lance was not thrown at an enemy or animal except in rare instances. It was used as a thrusting weapon by the Indian hunters or warriors —a protecting weapon or tool—much in the same manner as a modern soldier uses a bayonet on his rifle in combat.

Archaeologists in late years have found in scattered parts of the country evidence that the prehistoric hunting people used a tool called the atlatl or spear-launcher. This tool was used to throw flint-tipped darts or short spears. The atlatl was used to lengthen the arm of the thrower and to add force to the projectile when thrown. The atlatl was a stick a foot or more long with a hand grip at one end and a bone hook at the other to hold the base of the short spear or dart in place. This tool was used for throwing a short spear, in an overhand motion, with greater force than could be obtained by hand. We can assume that the length of the atlatl and weight of the flint-tipped spear or dart were governed by the range or distance desired and the size of the animal being hunted. Small darts or spears probably were used on small game, while larger ones were used on larger game where a harder striking force had to be used in bringing down the animal. During these times game probably was hunted at a close range. These hunters knew all the tricks of the trade, because their livelihood and existence depended on this type of hunting.

The size of these flint points varied greatly, indicating that these hunters probably had different sized points to use on their darts and short spears. In a sense they are arrow points, but they were not shot or propelled from bows as is generally believed.

Another hunting tool was the bola. A bola was a set of cords with egg-shaped stones (called plummets) tied on the ends of the cords. Spread out, the weapon looks like a pinwheel. When the hunter grasped the knotted ends of the strings and threw the device like a sling, the stones spread apart and whirled around; stunning small animals or birds or inmeshing them in the cords.

The hunters in their search for food probably also set fire to the grasslands and stampeded the game for the kill. They drove game over cliffs, dug pits, set traps or snares and used short spears for the kill. The hunters matched their wits, skill and strength against the fleetness and cunning of the wild beasts they hunted on foot.

These people of the late Archaic period who lived and hunted along the rivers, in the forests, and on the prairies made contacts with people in widely separated parts of the middle west. They traded, getting from distant places materials for weapons and hunting tools and objects for personal decoration. Granite stones found in glacial drifts furnished materials for stone axes. Deposits of flint in Indiana, Kentucky, Missouri, and Tennessee and the deposits in Union County, Illinois, furnished the raw materials that the skilled flint workers fashioned into hunting implements. Banded slate was obtained in trade from the south shores of Lake Huron and was used to make personal objects such as gorgets, pendants, and bannerstones.

Though some new types of tools and ornaments were developed during the late Archaic period, basically this culture remained the same from beginning to end. In this area their camping places are more numerous than those of succeeding Indian cultures, due mainly to their movements from place to place in search of food. Unlike other groups they built few mounds for their dead, so that their camp sites cannot always be found, because burial mounds are lacking.

3. Woodland Culture

A somewhat different culture, now known as the Woodland culture, began to evolve probably about three thousand years ago. These Indian groups spread out over the area, following the principal rivers and streams. The similarity of the flint and stone tools of both the late Archaic and early Woodland people suggests a connection or tie-in with people of both cultures; however, a gradual change was taking place, since one of these was making pottery.

Climatic conditions probably played a large part in this change, since the climate at this time was ideal, with ample moisture to sustain and create an abundant plant and animal life. As a result, game and fish were plentiful; thus it was unnecessary for the Indians to move about from place to place in search of food as they had done at an earlier time when game was scarce. They began to live in small villages and began to make pottery from local clays and tempered it with sand and grit to make it more durable.

The Woodland people are sometimes referred to as "stone boilers," because instead of always placing their fragile clay vessels in the fire, they often heated round pebble-like stones and placed them in the pots to cook or heat the food.

Since these people were becoming somewhat more settled than the previous Archaic people, agriculture was practiced to a limited extent. This, however, was probably no more than a garden-type farming, with only small plots of ground around their small villages. They depended to great extent on the seasonal natural resources, such as nuts, wild fruits, and the wild grass seeds, which they used as cereals to supplement a meat diet. Evidence can still be found throughout the area of many of their small villages and camping places. Some of their artifacts are still to be found near these places; their culture included only the implements necessary for hunting and for limited gardening.

They hunted with the spear and used the atlatl. Their hunting tools found today point to the fact that they were excellent workers in flint and stone; the projectile points, knives, and spearheads show excellent workmanship for the most part.[5]

The Woodland people, over a period of many centuries, formed separate cultural groups. In a time sequence these cultures are referred to as early, middle and late Woodland. Some of these local Indian cultural groups were given different names by archaeologists to distinguish them from other groups that once lived in the area. Some of these groups are now known as Red Ocher, Baumer, Crab Orchard, Hopewellian, Raymond, and Dillinger.

The Red Ocher people made burial mounds on low, natural ridges. Their mounds were some of the earliest in this area. They sometimes sprinkled powdered hematite on the bodies of their dead, a custom from which they drew their name Red Ocher.

A Woodland site in Massac County was excavated and studied about twenty-five years ago. This site was on the Baumer farm, and the Indians who at one time lived here are now referred to as the Baumer culture.

The Crab Orchard culture received its name from the fact that several Woodland sites were found and excavated a number of years ago near Crab Orchard Creek in Williamson County. The area where these sites were found and studied is now Crab Orchard Lake.

Other Woodland sites were found near the Big Muddy River north of Carbondale in Jackson County. The Raymond (Rieman) site on the Rieman farm is the older of the two. The Dillinger site on the Dillinger farm is a late Woodland site. Both of these Woodland sites were partly excavated and studied by archaeologists about twenty-five years ago.

The Baumer and Crab Orchard cultures are distinguished by pottery vessels made of grit or sand-tempered clay. Their vessels had flat bases or were long vessels with round bottoms. Though there is a great deal of similarity in these two cultures, there are some distinct differences in the pottery. The Crab Orchard artifacts include many flint articles and pottery type variations which are not found in the Baumer cultural materials. The

---

⁵The bevels on each side of some of the Archaic and Woodland points were once thought to have been made purposely to make the spear spin in flight—like a rifle bullet. This would be a disadvantage, as a wide flint point would not have the penetrating power when rotating. What really happened was that when the Indian hunter resharpened these points, they became beveled, and the more they were rechipped, the narrower and shorter they became. Many of these spear points probably were used also as knives that needed occasional sharpening on the cutting edges.

Baumer culture extended through the early Woodland period, while the Crab Orchard culture extended from early Woodland through the middle Woodland period. The ideas of the Crab Orchard culture appear to have been influenced by the Hopewellian people who came into the area somewhat less than two thousand years ago.

The Dillinger group that lived here showed the cultural influence of the Mississippi people also living in the area, approximately seven or eight hundred years ago. This Mississippi people probably introduced the bow and arrow to these Woodland people.

There are many Woodland sites along streams in the area. A large site was reported on the north side of the south fork of Saline River in Williamson County in 1949. This site has been investigated and is now known as the Jones site.

Historic Woodland Indian Tribes

The economy of the Woodland Indian tribes in the historic period was that of forest hunters, and though their women tended small plots of ground in the forests, raising squashes, corn, and beans, their agriculture never reached a higher stage than a garden-type farming, because no beasts of burden were used to cultivate crops.

The historic Woodland Indians lived in "wigwams" (an Algonquin term for "house"), made by setting in the ground poles bent into a dome shape, then covering them for added warmth in winter with slabs of bark and sometimes mats of cattails. Platforms around the sides served as sleeping and sitting places. The fire was in the center of the hard-packed earth floor; their food was cooked by dropping hot stones from the fire into the earthen pots.

Historians tell us that the clothing of the historic Woodland Indians was not elaborate; even in winter a man wore moccasins, leggings, a breechcloth, and a robe made of deerskins. Women wore skirts formed by folding a skin around the waist; sometimes they wore jackets for upper garments.

Although the Woodland people formed separate cultural groups, one common trait which continued into and throughout the Woodland period was a traditional form of burial. When a man died, his arms and legs were drawn up close to the head and he was buried in this position. This is known as a flexed or double-up burial.

When the historic, or late, Woodland Indian tribes were contacted by early explorers, they were still in the Stone Age, although they did have crude pottery. They had not advanced much farther than the prehistoric Woodland culture of twenty or more centuries before.

4. Hopewellian Culture

Because of social and economic necessity an Indian community hardly ever consisted of more than one hundred and fifty people (with the exception of the Mississippians). When the number reached beyond that limit, very often it became necessary for a part of the tribe to leave the parent group and move elsewhere. This splitting apart occurred in prehistoric times for thousands of years, and when the first explorers came they found the whole continent occupied by many different Indian tribal groups.

The question has often been asked, "Who were the Hopewellians?" Archaeologists have placed them in the general Woodland pattern, but their culture and way of life were in marked contrast to the Woodland culture at any time. Sometime between the early and middle Woodland periods a technological and social revolution seems to have taken place which resulted in a superior culture known as Hopewellian.

It is possible that by the time of the middle Woodland period there had been a fusion or mixture of several Woodland cultural groups, resulting in a hybrid type of people. Excavations and findings in some of their burial mounds in southern Illinois have shown among their skeletal remains round-headed as well as long-headed skulls, suggesting a mixture or fusion of at least two physical types.

Sometimes there is an evolution with the intermingling of two cultures, resulting in a new and superior culture or way of life. This may be the explanation to this prehistoric Hopewellian culture which was able to stay "on top" in cultural achievements for a few hundred years and then, for some unexplained reason, disappear.

It is hard to believe that this culture could disappear so completely, because it is known that it was highly developed. The people lived in large villages, began to farm, built tombs for their departed leaders (covered over with large mounds of earth), traded for objects (such as conch shells, mica, and copper ore from distant places), and became expert sculptors. One possible explanation for the disappearance of this group may be found in their complex, highly developed economy, which probably made them an easy target for more primitive and war-minded people.

First Hopewellian Finds

Archaeologists have known of the Hopewellian culture for over fifty years, but its presence in Illinois was not definitely established until a later time. Many people often ask, "Where did these Indians get the name Hopewellian?" and "Where did archaeologists first find evidence of these people?" Evidence of this culture was found about the year 1890, in Ohio. Dr. Warren K. Moorehead and other archaeologists, in excavating some mounds near Paint Creek, a stream in Ross County, Ohio, uncovered objects such as mica, copper ear spools, axes, obsidian (volcanic glass), shell work, and drilled fresh-water pearls. The mounds were on a farm owned by a Captain M. C. Hopewell; so, in honor of the owner of the land, they called this Indian culture Hopewellian.

When America was being settled west of the Alleghenies, along the Ohio River, the hunters and early settlers saw many Indian mounds. Intrigued by the mystery of the origin of these mounds, they spoke of the "mound-builders" whom they believed to be a race distinct from the Indians they were pushing westward. This concept has long ago been discredited by scientific evidence, which reveals that the builders of the mounds were the ancestors of the historic American Indians. However, the shifting within, the migrating from the region of different Indian cultural groups many centuries before, had left a time gap so wide that the historic Indians whom white men found living there knew no more about who had built these mounds than the first white men. We now know that some of these mounds were built by the Hopewellian Indians.

First Hopewellian Finds in Illinois

Evidence of the Hopewellian culture was found in Illinois in the year 1926. In Fulton County, a log tomb, enclosed in a mound, was uncovered which contained Hopewellian artifacts and skeletal remains. The first evidence of this culture in southern Illinois was found in 1945, when remains of several large villages were found near Gorham, in Jackson County. In Perry County, near Beaucoup Creek, a mound was excavated a number of years ago. This mound contained several burials, a number of copper ear spools, and several broken pottery vessels.

Other villages and mounds belonging to this culture have been found near the Wabash River in White County. One of the large mounds was excavated in 1950, and the village site was partly excavated the next year by a field party under the direction of the Illinois State Museum.

The emergence and duration of the Hopewellian culture in the Mississippi, Ohio, Illinois, and Wabash valleys cannot be determined by present evidence. It is known, however, that these people probably were already living in Illinois about two thousand years ago. It is only recently that material remains of charcoal, shell, and bone found in village sites have been dated by the "Carbon 14" method.[6] This new technique of dating prehistoric remains such as shell, bone or charcoal has been developed by physicists as a means of determining the approximate date of prehistoric materials. Based on the principle that all organic matter contains a measurable amount of radioactive isotopes of carbon, the rate of disintegration can be measured with a sensitive Geiger counter, and the age can be calculated. As the half-life of radioactive carbon is 5,560 years, this method is accurate within a small degree of experimental error.

---

[6]The "Carbon 14" dating of Indian remains has removed the guesswork in determining the age or time a site was occupied. The carbon test, with its margin for error limited to a few hundred years, has proven that Indians have lived here much longer than suspected a few years ago.

The method of comparing tree rings in logs and timbers used by the Indians to the rings of living trees, and thereby computing the date of the timber, has been unsuccessful in southern Illinois due to the lack of old trees in the area. However, at the Kincaid site, by comparing living tree rings to rings of logs excavated in the site, it was possible to establish a tentative date of a little over the year 1550 for the Mississippian culture at this site which followed the Hopewellian in southern Illinois.

Here in southern Illinois, the Hopewellians were busy trading up and down the river, farming, and becoming more settled in their habits centuries before the Roman Empire fell in A.D. 476. The paths of their migrations were along the river valleys. Excavations thus far have provided a number of facts and a still greater number of unanswered questions. They were, it seems, a peaceful, settled people who practiced some agriculture and who lived in villages in the river valleys. The type of house they lived in was oblong or rectangular and of the same general class as those constructed by the Woodland Indians.

Archaeological evidence found in their village sites suggests that the Hopewellian Indians were probably dominated by a ruling class and in contact with parent groups who traded with other Indians in villages miles apart. The materials from which they made their personal adornments, tools, and implements bear out the fact that they were travelers and traders. Sheet mica was brought from North Carolina to be used as mirrors and also cut into intricate and geometric designs. Small marine shells used for beads and large conch shells used for dippers and ladles came from Florida and the Gulf region. Some obsidian and grizzly-bear tusks were brought or traded from as far away as Yellowstone in the Rocky Mountains. Copper was brought from the Lake Superior region. The territory covered in passing on these ideas and in trading the raw materials for fashioned articles seems quite beyond the possibilities of aboriginal man, but early historians tell us of Indians who made long journeys and went to faraway places during their lives.

One often hears of the mysterious, "lost art of hardening copper" employed by the prehistoric Indians. They did not use any method to harden the copper implements but, instead, fashioned them from pure native nugget copper, the hardening coming from cold hammering and annealing. In this manner the implements did harden to a certain extent and would retain an edge better than smelted and cast copper.

All of these achievements made the Hopewellians, perhaps, the most advanced people of their time in America north of Mexico. The expressions on the faces found in their artistic stone carvings are known to be the best rendered with the exception of the last stages of the Mississippi culture of about the year 1500. The clay or terra cotta figurines of Hopewellian artists which have been found in this area are as lifelike as any prehistoric sculpturing ever discovered in the Mississippi or Ohio valleys. The fact that they probably are portraits of individuals makes them serve as a guide to the dress and personal appearance of these people, as they show plainly the style of hair dress and other customs of this period.

Unless one has seen some of their work, it is difficult to believe the extent to which these people had advanced as sculptors. It is true that the use of hard metals, except copper, was still unknown, and that all the work of shaping and fashioning had to be done with sharp pieces of flint. But sharp flint in the hands of a true artist can perform miracles. For example, the Maoris of New Zealand had never seen a single scrap of any sort of metal until the white man settled among them a hundred years ago, but the art of these people and their sculptured ornaments in wood and stone are excellent examples of the carver's art.

The greatness of the Hopewellians was due in part, probably, to their mythological philosophy, their rituals, and their high regard for their dead, for the soul of a people is reflected in what we call their mythology or beliefs—a combination of fiction, philosophy, mysticism, and ethics. These Indians expressed their religion in their art. They were probably devoted to things they observed around them: persons living and dead, legendary heroes, animals, and the external forces of nature, such as thunder, lightning, and fire, which were considered supernatural.

Many of the Hopewellian effigy pipes represent animals or the human face; however, most of their pipes were without ornamentation. We smoke for pleasure and from habit, but smoking by historic as well as prehistoric Indians was largely of a ceremonial nature. The practice of smoking was probably confined to the more important priests, such as the Shaman "medicine doctors," or some other important personages who may have believed that the work of evil spirits could be counteracted or appeased with the incense of this herb. This theory is borne out by the fact that very few of their pipes are found anywhere other than in tombs with the dead.

While information on the religious, social, and economic life of any prehistoric group of people is at best fragmentary, from the evidence so far found it appears that the Hopewellians were further advanced than some of the later historic Indians found living here at the time of the early French explorers. Elaborate log- and bark-covered tombs enclosed in earthen mounds are landmarks of their culture. In these tombs they buried the dead with their adornments and implements, probably with much ceremony. However, these mounds were built mainly for the nobility or ruling class, and other burials have been found in common graves (both in flexed and extended burials) with little or no grave goods. The nobility were usually buried in an extended position as we bury our dead today, while the common people were buried in a flexed position.

Unfortunately we know little about the ancient rituals that may have been connected with their burial ceremony, but we can be sure that they were well-developed. An aboriginal people who have developed a semi-sedentary culture will develop elaborate religious rites for the dead, partly because agriculture gives them leisure time which previously was required for hunting and migrating to new hunting grounds. It is probably because they practiced agriculture that they had more time to think about the mysteries of life and death than did more primitive people. While we marvel at their burial tombs and the pagan rituals that must have been employed in respect to the dead, perhaps we should remember that we, too, have elaborate funerals for our dead and erect monuments to them.

The Hopewellian mounds that have been excavated in southern Illinois contained beautifully fashioned artifacts such as beads, bonework, drilled bear tusks, copper ear spools, drilled pearls, sheet mica, and tools such as copper axes, conch-shell dippers, and pipes that had been placed with the dead.

The question next arises, "What happened to these people whose culture was so far advanced?" The only clues we have left today with which to study these people are the archaeological evidences we have found in their long-uninhabited village sites and their burial mounds. One clue to the disappearance of the Hopewellian way of life may be that after a time they were gradually assimilated by Woodland people living here or coming into the area in increasing numbers. At first the Hopewellians were probably able to carry on their traditions. But overwhelming numbers of Woodland Indians, after a time, probably compelled them to adopt many of the economic traits and ways of their neighbors.

After a period of time, we know, there was a waning of the Hopewellian ceremonial complex to an inferior one composed of Woodland cultural traits, with only remnants remaining of the high cultural complex they had brought with them. The abandonment of these Hopewellian traits gradually led to the adoption of the more primitive Woodland ways, including that of "no offering for the dead."

It is unlikely that these Indians disappeared without a trace. They must be represented in the ancestry of some of the historic tribes, but there are no legends or traditions among the historic Indians concerning them. All efforts to connect the Hopewellian culture with that of the historic tribes has so far ended in failure. To this day, we do not know who they were. Consequently, we are right back where everyone had ended up thus far—up a blind alley—because the mysterious riddle of the Hopewellians remains unexplained. Perhaps some day we shall collect enough evidence to answer this tantalizing puzzle.

5. Mississippi Culture

The Indians whose culture archaeologists now refer to as the Mississippi culture probably lived in the southeastern part of the United States, migrating westward into Louisiana, Alabama, Mississippi, and Tennessee. It appears, from present evidence, that some moved farther southeast into Georgia, while others came and settled in southern Illinois and adjoining areas. They probably arrived in this area over one thousand years ago, coming from Tennessee and Kentucky, and living here continuously until late in the sixteenth century.

They brought with them an advanced culture based on agriculture and lived in large villages and towns in the flood plains of the Mississippi and Ohio rivers and their tributaries. After coming here they carried on an exchange of ideas with people living farther south. Some of the artifacts we find suggest that they were in periodic contact with other people as far away as Mexico. Other traits and ideas such as building pyramidal (square-based), truncated (flat-topped) mounds as foundations for their temples or houses are good examples of borrowed ideas, probably from Mexico.

Religious ceremonies seem to have played a very important part in the lives of these people. They buried their dead in cemeteries along with pottry vessels containing food and with other personal items for an afterlife.

Their large villages were composed of hundreds of well-made houses of light poles set in the ground, with dirt floors, walls plastered over with clay mixed with grasses, and roofs covered with this mixture over which bundles of grass were laid close together, fastened down, and overlapping enough to shed water.

In the center of their village was a plaza or play court. Here different kinds of games were played. One game that was played is called "chunky." Disklike stones called discoidals, generally concave on both sides, were used and are often found in the areas of these old play courts in their village sites.

Some of their towns were walled or surrounded with a palisade made of vertical posts set close together and plastered over with wattle, a mixture of clay and grasses. This wall probably was high enough so that a person would have a difficult time climbing over it. Investigations and surface observations of one of these walls show that guard stations existed at about sixty-foot intervals on the inside. A moat or ditch on the outside of the terrace on which the wall was built extended the full length of the wall. This moat probably contained water most of the year and was an aid in keeping out other Indians living nearby or passing through the area on raids.

The large town at Cahokia mounds near East St. Louis and others in the flood plains of southern Illinois were, because of their size, probably the dominating cultural centers of these people.

The Mississippians used the bow and arrow as their chief weapons in hunting and warfare. By combining hunting and the gathering of wild fruits and nuts, they learned to improve their environment with agriculture. This alone made it possible for them to build towns and homes and live here for many years. Many interested people asked the question, "Why did these Indians build on the flood plains of rivers that sometimes overflowed and flooded the valleys?" They did so because farming was the most important means of providing food, and valleys afforded them every comfort. Here the rich soil was easily worked and planted—they were farmers and knew good earth when they saw it. The hot, moist river valleys in summer were good for raising tobacco, sunflowers, beans, maize, squash, and other vegetable crops. Their corn or maize was planted in irregularly spaced bunches as well as in straight rows as we plant it today. Since they had no draft animals, such as horses or oxen, to use in their farming operations, all cultivation of their crops had to be done by hand, using only flint and shell hoes with wooden handles. This makes the advanced state of their culture more amazing. These village farmers stored crops for later use, thereby insuring economic security for themselves. Under the influence of plant husbandry these people built homes and lived simple, free lives close to nature.

They lived in villages and theirs was an agricultural community, and their rituals were probably rooted in agriculture. The planting and harvesting rituals were probably the outstanding ceremonies of the year. These were held in appreciation of the corn, squash, and beans they were able to grow and store to feed themselves during the winter and until the harvesting of the next crop.

Cultural Achievements

Industries, such as the utilization of the flint quarried for tools and implements, the utilization of clay in their ceramics or pottery-making, the tanning of hides for clothing, the evaporation of brine from salt springs to crystal salt, and the development of agriculture made their culture more advanced than that of any of the Indian groups before or after them until the coming of the white man.

Due to their semi-sedentary way of life, pottery-making reached its highest development with the Mississippians. They were the best potters in the Mississippi Valley in prehistoric Indian times. Most of their pottery was utilitarian and served the everyday needs of cooking and storing food. The color was buff, gray, or black, depending on the type of firing in the open hearths. On some of their vessels red ocher was painted or rubbed on their pottery, giving it a red color. Crushed mussel shell was added to temper the clay before it was fired. Since the potter's wheel was unknown in this area, in prehistoric times, all pottery was made by hand. The larger vessels sometimes show the imprints of loosely woven netting or plaited fiber on the underside, which are probably marks from the mold or from the form in which the clay was placed when the vessel was being made. There were many forms and styles of jars, pots, bowls, bottles, plates, and cuplike vessels. Most of these were plain; others were effigies representing mammals, fishes, birds, and humans. Many of the bowls were shaped like kettles, with handles or loops on the side. Sometimes small effigy figures of animals were molded on the rim for handles or simply for decorating the vessel.

Ceramics was only one of the arts of the Mississippi people. Though their pipes were sometimes made of pottery, most of them were stone effigy pipes, up to six inches high. These pipes were generally carved with figures representing the human form in a sitting or squatting position. Fluorspar was used by some of the Mississippians living near the Ohio River, where this mineral is being mined today. They carried on quite an industry carving and working this material into beads, pendants, earplugs, and other ornaments. *Repoussé* work in sheet copper and figures etched on shell ornaments, suggesting Mexican or southern influence, have also been found in their graves in southern Illinois.

The designs and symbols the Mississippians used are many and varied and include the equal-arm cross, the spider, the serpent, the scalloped disk design or sun symbol, and dancing figures. A spider as a basis for ornamental design is not strange when we consider that it was from the spider that the Indian was supposed to have learned of weaving. Thus, the spider would be held in high esteem. The serpent played an important part in the ceremonial life of these Indians, which may account for the fact that the serpent or rattlesnake design must have had special significance in mythology; scalloped disk designs indicating a circle or sun symbol suggest sun worship. Many of these designs are firmly entrenched in their art traditions. As symbols, carved designs were intended to possess a religious character, and when worn as amulets they were supposed to have supernatural protective power. Many of their objects were inscribed with mythological characters, while other displayed geometric designs only.

When the word "pyramid" is mentioned, one probably does not think of Illinois; most people think they must go to Egypt or to Mexico to see pyramids, or to the Near East to see ruined cities, but both are within the borders of this state. Our pyramids are not of stone; they are of earth. Yet, the archaeological treasures are practically as rich as those in Egypt. Every visible trace of the ruined towns is gone and only by careful excavating can archaeologists reconstruct the picture of earth floors and the outlines of the post holes left from the original houses, yet the stories these outlines tell are as intriguing as those of Egypt. The mounds and village remains in the flood plains are landmarks of the Mississippian culture.

The rectangular earth mounds were not built as high places of refuge from ancient floods but some were earth foundations for temples of wood with mud-plastered walls, which were erected possibly to reflect the Indians' appreciation of the sun for the harvest it provided. The custom of fire worship might also have been practiced at this time, as hard-packed clay altars have been found near the tops of some of the larger mounds on which there is still evidence of fire hearths or fireplaces. Some historic Indians had a ceremony of keeping the sacred fire burning in their temple or council house for a year and then extinguishing it, after which another fire was begun in the "New Fire Ceremony."

The Creek Indians who lived farther south held a ceremony

to celebrate their New Year after the corn had ripened. They cleaned their houses, burned all their old discarded clothing, tools and weapons, replacing them with new. The fires in the houses of the village were extinguished and the hearths were sprinkled with white sand. Then the most important rite of the festival began: the lighting of the New Fire. In the town square or plaza, four large logs were placed on the ground to form a cross with the outer ends facing the direction of the four cardinal points. At daybreak the fire maker facing the rising sun lighted the bundle of dried grass, moving it from east to west, and as it burst into flame he placed it in the center of the four logs, lighting the New Fire. The villagers sang songs while dancing around the fire, and at the conclusion of the ceremonies each woman in the village was given an ember from the New Fire to take to her home to relight her own hearth. It was in this manner that the Creek Indians began their New Year, thankful for the harvest and purified for the days ahead.

Cahokia Mounds

The greatest group of earth mounds in this country, if not in the world, is called Cahokia Mounds. Today a part of the area including twelve of the mounds has been set aside as Cahokia Mounds State Park. Here the Indians once built a mound larger than the great pyramid Cheops, built in Egypt many centuries before.

Here on the flood plain of the Mississippi River, near East St. Louis, Illinois, are about eighty mounds. Monk's Mound, the largest of these mounds, was named for a group of Trappist monks who built a monastery on its top years ago. It is interesting to note that these devout men of the Christian religion built a monastery as a monument to their God on the top of a monument probably built, with so much labor, to the sun god of the Indians. The mound is so large that a person seeing it for the first time can hardly believe it to be man-made. It rises in four terraces to a height of one hundred feet and covers sixteen acres, an area larger than that covered by the largest Egyptian pyramid. Engineers have calculated that it took the labor of over a thousand people working many years to build this great monument. The political organization of the Mississippians must have been high to release so much time from the necessary work of getting food and other necessities of life.

Kincaid Mounds

In the extreme southeastern part of Illinois, in the Black Bend of the Ohio River, there is another large village site and group of mounds called Kincaid after a family who once owned the land. They have been explored and partly excavated by archaeologists from the University of Chicago. At this place one can see many mounds of various sizes. One mound has a two-acre base and is thirty feet high.

The Mississippi people were sometimes buried in mounds and in cemeteries on high bluffs. Contrary to popular opinion, their mounds were not built as monuments to the dead but served as sites for buildings and places of worship, where ceremonial rites were probably held. They also used the stone cist or vault burial in disposing of their dead. Slabs of stones were set on edge in a shallow grave and the body placed therein and covered over by slabs of rock. Bundle burials also have been found. In such cases it appears that the bodies had been placed on a scaffold or in a tree until the flesh had decayed, and then the bones were gathered up in a bundle and buried. This was a common practice of the historic Indians, especially on the western plains. Often archaeologists find adult skeletons with artifically deformed heads, which resulted from the binding of the head during infancy to a cradle board. This was a common practice of Woodland, Hopewellian, and Mississippian peoples. Often children of the Mississippi people were buried in the dirt floor of the homes. With the coming and going of different cultures, burial styles changed, just as in our lifetime coffins which were formerly made of wood are now made of metal and bronze, and cement and marble vaults have come into use.

Ferdinand de Soto, the Spanish explorer, and his footsore cavaliers arrived at the lower Chickasaw bluffs overlooking the Mississippi River (not far from the present city of Memphis, Tennessee) early in May in the year 1541, over four centuries ago. Here they found a large Indian population awaiting their arrival. They were living in organized communities, and sometimes their villages were sentry-patrolled, fortified and protected by palisades of high, sharp-pointed tree trunks set close together. These Indians were a sturdy people with black hair and dark eyes and with yellow-brownish skins, painted or tattooed.

If the explorers had come further north up the river at this time, they would have found the same kind of Indians living along the Ohio and Mississippi rivers that border southern Illinois and across these rivers in Missouri, Kentucky, and Indiana.

Sites such as those at Wickliffe and Tolu, Kentucky; the Angel Mounds near Evansville, Indiana; the Kincaid Mounds all along the Ohio River, and Cahokia Mounds and others in southern Illinois along the Mississippi River were still inhabited by these Indians at this time.

This culture, the culmination or climax of over ten thousand years of prehistoric Indian occupation in that area, had disappeared by the time the French explorers came late in the seventeenth century. Archaeologists have never agreed on the explanation or reason for the disappearance of this culture. A theory has been advanced that they were overrun and destroyed by the less cultured Woodland Indians about five hundred years ago. There is no evidence to support the idea that warfare was the cause, yet the question, however, still remains unanswered as to why De Soto, in 1541, encountered a large population of settled people along the lower Mississippi River, while Marquette found only a fragmentary population in 1673, or 132 years later. By the time of Marquette's voyage in 1673, and La Salle's voyage in 1682, the entire population along the lower Mississippi River was less than the number of people in one of the small rural towns of today. The French explorers were amazed by the absence of Indians along this great river. It seemed to them a more primitive wilderness than that along the Atlantic coast. There is no mention made in explorers' accounts of a great concentration of Indians in the East St. Louis-Collinsville area at this time. The great Mississippian Indian site at Cahokia Mounds had long been engulfed in tall grass. Brackenridge,[7] an early observer, gave a

---

[7]H. M. Brackenridge, "Views of Louisiana," quoted by A. J. Conant in *Footprints of Vanished Races* (St. Louis: Chancy R. Barns, 1879), p. 27.

vivid description of the Cahokia Mounds in the year 1811, when the whole landscape was covered with wild grass. He was astonished by the quantity of human bones dug up everywhere, or found on the surface of the ground.

Many theories have been advanced concerning the fact that some of the village sites appear to have been destroyed by fire. This, however, is probably not what caused the disappearance of the Indians. Though the survivors may have burnt the village sites to appease the angry gods or spirits for some disaster that had befallen them, it would only have been a short time after the villages were deserted for any reason before a common grass fire could have burnt down their remaining houses, obliterating all outward traces. The finding of outlines of palisades or upright posts supported by earthen embankments built around some of their towns supports the idea that all was not well with their neighbors. There is one large village site in the southwestern part of Union County, near Clear Creek, and another at the Kincaid Mounds, near the Ohio River, in Massac County, where there are traces of stockades and embankments built around the towns for protection.

A more tenable theory is that they may have fallen victim to new diseases introduced by the early Spanish explorers in 1541, for in the wake of Spanish exploration came pestilence. We now know that the deadliest weapons brought by white man to the Indians were his diseases. One of these dreaded diseases was smallpox. The Spaniards first brought smallpox into Mexico in the early part of the sixteenth century, and within a short period thereafter three and one half million Indians died of the disease. It probably spread northward and some of the Indian tribes along the New England coast were stricken by the epidemic just prior to the landing of the Pilgrims in the *Mayflower*. There are historic accounts of smallpox killing over sixty million people in Europe in the eighteenth century, so it is not hard to imagine the danger it would have presented to the Indians' existence.

If centers such as the Cahokia Mounds, Kincaid, and other places in the area were still occupied by the Mississippi people as late as the year 1541, and there is reason to believe that they were, this smallpox epidemic may have spread northward and weakened them to the extent that the survivors were forced to leave the area or merge with the less-cultured Woodland people. Disease, probably more than any other factor, seems to have brought on the decline and disappearance of the Mississippi culture.

It now appears from archaeological investigations that possibly a century before the first French explorations there were no large Indian towns in existence in southern Illinois. Most of the tribes were living in the north along the Illinois River. After the Spanish exploration in the south, in 1541, this southern area was a vast hunting ground—a sort of "no man's land"—with only a few dispersed, small Indian villages.

The prehistoric Indians whose "footprints" the archaeologists follow are the ancestors of the Indian of today. Of these early cultures, the groups which perished and the ones whose ancestral lines remained are more or less mysteries. It is now thought that the fusion or intermingling of these early cultures—Archaic, Woodland, Hopewellian, and Mississippian—produced hybrid mixtures in varying combinations. Some of these mixtures were the historic Indian tribes which French explorers found living here.

6. Culture of the Historic Indians

De Soto's expedition in 1541, over four centuries ago, encountered many Indian villages on the lower Mississippi River. These villages were inhabited by Indians belonging to the great Muskhogean family including the Creek, the Choctaw, the Chickasaw, the Seminole, and the Natchez Indians. Since these Indians are so similar to the prehistoric Mississippi Indians, it is possible that they were a part of a large migration that reached into and beyond the Illinois country.

The Natchez tribe of the Muskhogean family were typical of all the tribes of this great family. These people worshiped the sun; they also kept a perpetual fire burning in their temples.

As we think of them today, theirs was not a democratic society, as there were two classes of people, the commoners and the nobles. The ruler was the king, or Great Sun, who had absolute power over the lives of his subjects. When he died, all his wives were executed and buried with him. In the Natchez society it was possible for a woman to become the Great Sun, or ruler, and enjoy the same power and privileges as a king.

The Natchez were similar to the Mississippians, and from them we can find a great deal to fill in the stories and explain the customs of the Mississippians and the artifacts found in their towns and burial grounds. Their traditions referred to their coming from the southwest. They were superior to all their neighbors; their language was different; and their political organization high. When the explorers found them, they were building on artificial mounds in the flood bottoms near the Mississippi River.

The houses of the Natchez Indians were well made, the majority being rectangular in shape and built so as to be cool in summer and warm in winter. The walls were made by setting posts in the ground at close intervals, weaving flexible sticks or reeds horizontally to the eaves, and plastering the whole wall with mud mixed with grasses. The roofs were covered with bundles of grass fitted so closely together that they made good insulation and shed water easily. The floors were made of hard-packed, smoothed clay. Inside each house was a fireplace or hearth on the floor, used for cooking and for heat in winter. There were no windows, and a single hole in the roof was an escape for the smoke from within. Each house was used by at least a dozen or more people, who slept on skins on the floor or on low bunks near the walls. The explorers found that farming was a major occupation of these southern tribes.

Maize, sunflowers, squash, beans, and tobacco were raised in quantity. Squash, corn, and beans were their main crops. A mixture of corn removed from the cob and beans is known as succotash. These Indians wore little clothing. Cotton and hemp were woven into coarse cloth on crude looms. Net webs covered on both sides with overlapping turkey, swan, and duck feathers were made into jackets or outer garments. The Natchez excelled in tanning and dressing hides and skins, and were artists in the use of dyes. They often painted the clothing which they wore with mineral paint and vegetable dye mixed with water and oil made from nuts, sunflowers, and animal fat. The art of these tribes, especially the ceramic art of the Natchez, was similar to that found in southern Illinois in the graves of the Mississippi people.

B. Indian Culture Before the White Man

1. Languages and Dialects

When first discovered, what is now the United States contained more than two thousand tribes comprising nearly one million Indians. The Indian population at the present time in the United States has been estimated at 343,500. Contrary to popular opinion, they are not a dying race, but are increasing in numbers.

Nothing is known about the languages of the prehistoric Indians; since they had no written language, their speech is lost in antiquity. When the white man discovered this continent, these two thousand Indian tribes spoke some two hundred and forty languages and over six hundred dialects. Today two hundred and fifty different languages and dialects are spoken by American Indians—more than all the languages spoken in Asia and Europe. Since they were not written, the languages changed so rapidly that in a few generations after a group split they could not understand each other. In such a manner, new dialects were born.

Difference in language, however, was not a great barrier to the Indians; they could make themselves understood by the use of sign language. In some cases, groups of Indians with the same language had different cultures, or groups of Indians with the same culture spoke different languages.

Couriers or messengers were often sent from village to village to call tribes to council or war. Bundles made of different paraphernalia depicting the event were sometimes the only means of sending messages and readily understood by all. Sometimes smoke signals, relayed from the high elevations, were used. Signals were sent by means of controlled smoke, and at night blinking fire was used. Messages could be sent hundreds of miles in a short time. This type of communication was the forerunner of our modern telegraph and was almost as efficient.

2. Transportation

Distances between groups of people may have fostered differences in languages and dialects. The dugout canoe, which was one of the earliest types of craft for water travel, and which was being used long before white men discovered America, was the only means of transportation other than by human transport until the introduction of the horse in the historic period. On overland treks the Indians themselves, for centuries, had carried all their goods and possessions. Early traders living among the Indians have observed that Indian women could carry more on their backs than most white men.

Romantic legends would have us believe that prehistoric Indians paddled up and down the rivers and streams in southern Illinois in birchbark canoes. We know that the birchbark canoe was made and used by the historic Indian tribes who lived in the northeastern part of the United States and along the Great Lakes. The source for making birchbark canoes was located in that area. It is doubtful, however, that the Indians in this area ever found birchbark in sheets large enough for canoe building. Birchbark canoes were used in this area, but only to a limited extent. Because they had to be brought into this area from the northeast, their use was not as widespread as is generally assumed.

The Indians who lived in southern Illinois and adjacent areas manufactured their dugout boats from trees growing in this area. They selected such trees as cottonwood, poplar, cypress, or soft maple, then stripped off the bark and hollowed out the logs with stone chisels and fire. The construction and types of boats differed with the locality because of the difference in woods used. A dugout made of a large log had several paddles and could be propelled through the water at great speed. Many of these, because of their large size, could carry as many as twenty or more people along with their provisions.

It has never been established as to what extent dugout boats were used in southern Illinois during the Archaic period. Since it is thought that there were no large forests in this area at that time, the only possible material for boat construction would have had to come from large cypress trees which were probably growing in the swamplands at the southern tip of Illinois. A study of the camping places or "stations" around the fringe of this once-vast swampland indicates that some travel was done by boat in this area by the early hunters and fishermen.

3. Primitive Medicine

Almost every religion had its beginning through the miracle

of healing. The most frequent request of mankind through the ages has been the plea for help in conquering sickness and disease. The Indians felt that the basic cause of an illness originated in the spirit world; their ideas of sickness were simple and they knew little or nothing of the symptoms of different diseases.

Some Indians claimed to be able to contact the spirit world through visions; there were, however, few individuals whose visions and experiences fitted them for the role of the medicine man. These few gifted persons' lives were dedicated to the task of gaining power over the evil that existed in the unseen world. They also had a knowledge of certain curative herbs and nothing more. The curing of the sick was only a faith cure, accomplished by the strength of faith received from the encouragement of the medicine man.

Today in the field of modern psychosomatic medicine, this curing becomes much easier to believe and understand, because the medicine man brought hope, understanding and confidence to his patient. These elements in some respects proved as powerful as any modern medicine. Without the sick man's will to live, few modern medicines have much effect. The suggestive power of the medicine man's magic was the essence of his ability to cure the sick.

In modern medical practice many old techniques and remedies have been discontinued. Within the memory of people still living, blood-letting was a common practice among doctors, who used this method on their patients afflicted with chronic-type blood diseases. The use of leeches, blood-sucking aquatic worms, was common in treating swellings resulting from bruises not many years ago.

Just as early Indian cultures are distinguished by methods of transportation, they are also distinguished by the primitive medicine which was practiced. Although we have no way of knowing which plants and herbs were used by the prehistoric Indians, we do know that the historic Indians used various plants and healing herbs. Even if miracle drugs were unknown to them, modern medicinal herbs were universally used by all Indians. Indians living east of the Mississippi River knew the curative power of wintergreen (acetyl salicylate), which we now know as aspirin, and many other herbs from which modern medicine is derived. A few of the medicinal herbs used by the Indians were bloodroot, wild cherry, slippery elm bark, coltsfoot, may apple, catnip, sage, peppermint, blackberry, flagroot, mullein, licorice, juniper and white-oak bark.

The Indian medicine men who were specialists in ritual were thought to possess supernatural powers and thus were held high in esteem by their fellow men. These medicine men, who have been ridiculed for many years, used antics, tricks, and noises to "drive away the evil spirit of pain." The doctor was not a fraud if he convinced the patient that he was on the road to recovery; it was the "art of suggestion" carried to a high point. These witch doctors succeeded, beyond expectations, in their healing.

4. Mythology

We remember from our schooldays the mythology of ancient Greece and Rome. A myth is a magical tale, true or false, which deals with the life of some important person. It is something that holds a curiously fascinating quality for all people, because it is a description of the unconscious wishes and superstitions, not only of the individual, but of whole groups of people. The universal similarity of myths in widely separated parts of the world had long been noted by anthropologists.

If a story grips us, the chances are strong that it contains mythical elements which appeal to our subconscious minds. The legendary story "The Song of Hiawatha" by Longfellow is an example of a mythical Indian figure in American literature. Through the medium of myth, many of our present-day ideas and beliefs have been handed down to us through the years from our ancestors of long ago.

One concrete example is the decoration of the fir or hemlock tree at Christmas time. We do not have to search far to find that this ceremony first originated with the Germans in Northern Europe long before they had ever heard of the Christian religion.

The spirit or soul of a people, primitive or civilized, is embodied in their beliefs. Wherever primitive people have lived in the world, superstition and spiritual mythology have developed in the minds of these people in an effort to solve the mysteries of nature. The creation of mythological heroes and figures in the legends and folklore of primitive people had a great impact on their way of life. There are yet living in remote sections of the world people such as the Australian bushman, savage headhunters of the upper Amazon River in South America, and natives of New Zealand and parts of Africa who have in their possession a large amount of ceremonial paraphernalia: idols, fetish objects, masks, legends, songs, and dances of a spiritual nature, which are of great importance in the minds and physical make-up of their people.

Archaeologists have found evidence to support the theory that mythology played an important part in the lives of the prehistoric Indians. Copper plates and shell ornaments have been found, incised, depicting mythological characters. The mythology of the Indians was based on older forms of nature worship practiced by all primitive people, in which natural phenomena were held in awe or in high esteem. In Indian life the religion and ceremonial rites were built around mythological heroes and legends. The storyteller was an important personage in their lives, especially to the young children. Many hours were spent recounting to children the deeds and exploits of importance of chiefs and persons no longer living. Sometimes mythological characters or spirits were invented, and as the story was repeatedly told, it became a legend lasting many years.

The mythological god of the old Norsemen was Thor. If you could have asked an ancient Scandinavian, "Who is God?" his reply would have been, "Thor, the god of battle and plunder." These old warriors loved such a deity.

5. Religion

It is a natural instinct among people, civilized or otherwise, to hope for an afterlife. Long before the Christian era the Pharaohs who ruled the Egyptians nearly five thousand years ago believed in a hereafter.

The ancient Egyptian believed that not only his spirit but his whole ego would live on after his earthly existence ended, and that his life beyond the grave was to be an exalted version of his life on earth.

A Pharaoh called Khufu believed the "solar boat" placed in his tomb would be useful as his servants rowed him through the heavens on his eternal journey.

The conception of a "spirit world" seems to be a natural trait that has been carried down through the ages by people in different parts of the world. Even among aboriginal people the belief of an afterlife removed much of the natural fear of death.

Evidence of a belief in an afterlife has been found in the mounds and graves of Indians in prehistoric America. The Hopewellian Indians, as has already been described, were burying the dead with their personal possessions in tombs, enclosed in mounds of earth, around two thousand years ago in southern Illinois and elsewhere in the Ohio and Mississippi valleys.

The most striking expression of these ideas was the inclusion of their material possessions which they loved and used in their everyday life while on earth. Among some Indian groups and tribes in prehistoric times the weapons, tools, ornaments and pottery were "killed" or broken before they were placed in the grave. The idea was to release the spirit of the object so that it could follow the soul of the departed person on his journey to the spirit world. Like the ancient Egyptians, the Hopewellian Indians erected large conoidal mounds over the tombs of their dead. However, in the case of the Hopewellians, it was earth instead of stone; nevertheless the motive was the same. The building of these mounds as monuments to the dead was done at enormous cost to the living, in time and labor involved.

The Mississippi Indians also included personal possessions in the graves with their dead; this custom continued into the historic period. Many historic Indian tribes followed this practice after the coming of white men.

The Indian idea or belief was that they would need their tools and weapons in the spirit world or the "happy hunting ground," where good Indians went when they died.

The religious beliefs of many Indian tribes were of a noble and exalted character, comparing favorably in their simplicity with great myths of other people living in different parts of the world. The religion of the Indians is not comparable to our present-day religious practices but was a part of their day-to-day life and was concerned with such matters as food-getting and social occasions, where ceremonies with rites were used. It was strong, dynamic, and inseparable from the rest of their way of life, and not just ritual habits. When Indians danced, it was to express their ideas and emotions.

All Indians had enough intelligence to partake in spiritual thinking. Some practiced it more than others, but an aboriginal people without a religion would be an unnatural thing indeed. The sincerity of the Indian is unquestioned when it comes to his beliefs and strict observance of the ceremonies and traditions of his people. The Indians were, on a whole, much more sincere in the worship of their deities than civilized people are in their religious practices.

The Indians' custom of meeting for their religious ceremonies every year or oftener was probably more or less like our family reunions. Our pioneer forefathers had their camp meetings, where the community would gather to feast and visit. Here they could express their feelings by singing and listening to a minister. These emotional experiences gave them strength to continue their way of life, which was rugged when compared with the way we live today.

Some of the rites and ceremonies that the Indian practiced would seem ridiculous to us, but many of the rites still used in secret fraternities and organizations of the present day seem just as ridiculous. The shrines, the images, the crucifixes, and the pictures before which some Christians worship have seemed to some idolatrous, but to many a supposed idolater they mean something else altogether. These are nothing more than aids to the imagination of the worshiper. In the same way, the things the Indians worshiped—the sun, the thunder, and the like— were only representations of their idea of God.

One of the outstanding features of Indian psychology was faith. They believed that their Gods were infallible and never lost faith in their own religion and their own deities. If things went wrong they blamed the evil spirits. At heart the Indian was a true spiritualist; when he removed himself from others by fasting, he was practicing his religion.

In our Christian religious practices faith is one of the fundamental doctrines.

The religious beliefs of many of the historic Indian tribes followed the same general idea of all other religious creeds. Many of their beliefs were in regard to the creation and accounted for the origin of the earth, the sea, the stars, animal and plant life, and for the presence of man. For them, all was controlled by some mighty personage who lives in the great beyond. Their ceremonies and rituals were to appease this Great Spirit. In the concept of an afterlife, to be found in the legends and traditions, the spirit lived in a future state and had a great distance to travel after death toward the west or setting sun. The phrase "gone west," often used today when a person dies, is of Indian origin. The Indians had a superstitious fear of animals and of the phenomenal workings of nature. In some tribes the myths are systematized in the form of a well-developed ritual. Some attempts have been made to prove that the Indians were atheistic. However, the legends and customs of some of the historic tribes prove otherwise. Everything was a solemn ritual to the Indian; every living thing, every blade of grass that moved in the wind, was to him the doings of the Great Spirit.

6. Traditions

Tradition has always been the enemy of progress, because primitive people will naturally preserve and carry forward their ancient beliefs. Myth and rituals often act as brakes upon the speed of cultural change, and this is one of the main reasons for the backwardness and slow progress of isolated groups of people. Aboriginal people are far more conscious of the role of cultural traits, or tribal customs, and less willing to accept change than people of our present modern civilization. Even today, we still find people who are afraid to break old habits and accept new ideas. As in Indian times, it is the older folks who are less apt to discard the *Volksgedanken,* or folk ideas, of their generation.

In aboriginal Indian times the children learned only from their parents or other adult members of the family or clan. Boys were taught at a very early age how to hunt and fish, because their lives depended upon it. The girls learned to gather food and prepare it and to take the skins from the animals the hunters brought in and to tan them and fashion them into clothing.

There was no outside influence to change their minds, and the introduction of ideas of other people they came in contact with was not of sufficient importance to change their way of life.

Some parents today are afraid to restrain their children for fear of giving them a lifelong complex. In some Indian tribes, the Indian parents refrained from punishing their children, because their creed was to respect any person's right to be an individual, and that a child should be taught by example, not by coercion. Some Indian parents felt that if they taught the child the right way of life, they had done their duty, and were not to blame if the child chose to go wrong. It is a matter of opinion whether this type of education has worked out very well for either the Indian or white man.

In contrast, in our civilization we attend school to study and learn new ideas, which we apply in our everyday living and in teaching others. In our daily contact with the outside world, we learn how other people live and adapt their practices to our own use.

During the lifetime of people living today, there has been a more rapid cultural change than ever before in the world. The shift from horsepower to the gasoline engine (automobiles and tractors) is a basic change in our cultural pattern. The diesel engine is rapidly replacing the old steam locomotive on our railroads and the latter will soon pass completely from the American scene. New gadgets make their appearance on the market every day; styles of clothing and automobiles change with the season; and our whole culture has become accustomed to changes.

In prehistoric Indian times, changes in houses, clothing, hunting tools, and implements came about very slowly and probably were not even noticed in the lifetime of an individual. The hunting tools of all the early Indians were spears, and, contrary to modern belief, it was thousands of years before the bow and arrow were introduced. When white men came, they found the Indians using the bow as well as the spear or lance.

Soon after white men came to trade and live, the Indians found it necessary to acquire guns to protect themselves from other Indians who had already obtained guns from the white men further east. The Iroquois from the northeast, who made

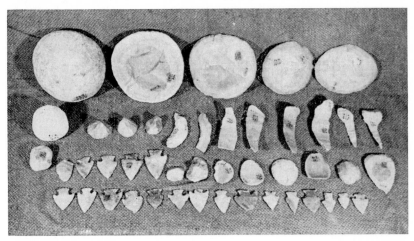

Irvin M. Peithmann

Nodular flint balls; in the upper left is a flint ball; the four others in the top row are disks made from flint balls by the percussion method using a hammer-stone. The other objects are knives, scrapers and projectile points made from flakes by pressure, using a bone flaking tool.

Banner stones of the archaic cultural period. All are from Southern Illinois archaic Indian sites.

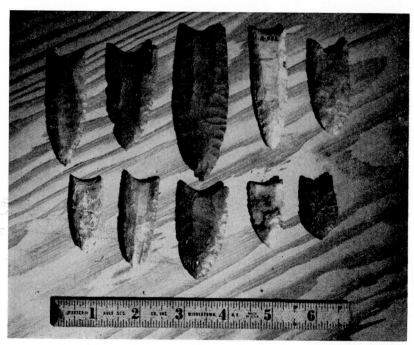

Irvin M. Peithmann

Fluted projectile points found in southern Illinois.

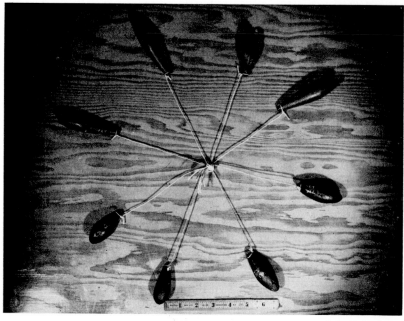

Irvin M. Peithmann

Showing probable use of plummets as a bola or hunting tool.

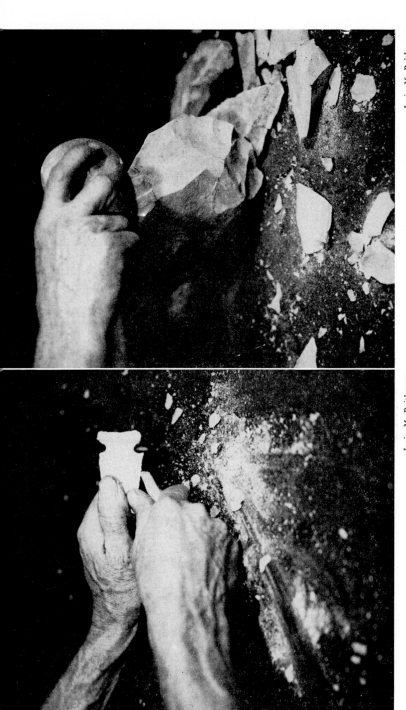

Pressure method showing how flakes were pressed off in the process of making a flint spear point.

Showing percussion method, with use of hammerstone to reduce large, flat flint nodules to shape and size in the manufacture of flint hoes and spades.

Hopewellian artifacts, southern Illinois: (1) pottery vessel, (2) clay statuette, (3) bone awls, (4) effigy frog pipe and plain pipes, (5) copper axes, (6) projectile points, (7) flint core, (8) flint knives, (9) flint flakes used as knives, (10) flint scrapers, (11) flint digging tools, (12) flint disks.

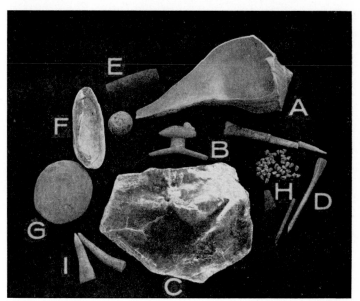

Artifacts from Hopewellian mound in the Dogtown hills near the Wabash River, White County, Illinois: (A) conch shell made into a dipper, (B) effigy duck pipe, (C) sheet mica, (D) bone awls, (E) tube pipe, (F) mussel-shell spoon, (G) worked stone, (H) shell beads, (I) antler tips.

Diorama in Illinois State museumobile depicting Hopewellian Indian throwing a spear with an atlatl or spear launcher.

This large Indian mound is a familiar sight to travelers along highway Route 3 in West Jackson County, Illinois. It is on the Cliemann farm.

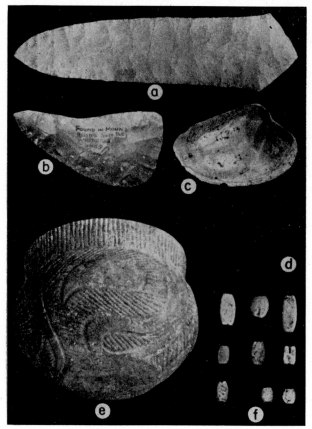

Artifacts from Hopewellian burial mound near the Wabash River, White County, Illinois: (a) flint knife, (b) flint knife, (c) mussel-shell spoon, (d) marine-shell beads, (e) incised pottery vessel.

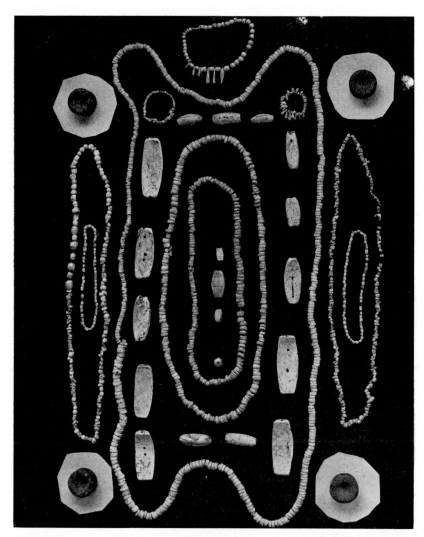

Bone, shell and pearl beads, and copper ear spools from Hopewellian burial mound near Gorham, Jackson County, Illinois.

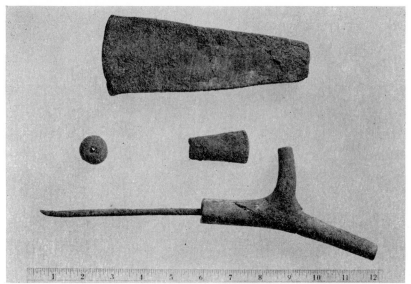

Copper objects found with skeletons in Hopewellian tomb: (*top*) copper ax, (*center left*) copper bead, (*center right*) small copper ax, (*bottom*) copper chipping tool with antler handle attached.

Hopewellian tomb containing seven skeletons and grave goods, in large mound near Wabash River, White County, Illinois, excavated under direction of Illinois State Museum, University of Chicago and Southern Illinois University, 1950.

Cast of clay statuette, or figurine; original found near
Gorham, Jackson County, Illinois, and now in Illinois
State Museum at Springfield.

Hopewellian plain platform pipe.

*Sketched by Russell Peithmann
from photo by J. Grider*

Motif depicting a man playing chunky with a stone discoidal.

Sketch showing how the people of the Mississippi culture constructed their houses. The walls were plastered over with clay mixed with grasses, and the roofs were covered with this mixture over which bundles of grass were laid close together, fastened down, and overlapped enough to shed water. A fire hearth in the center dug into the dirt floor with an escape hole in the roof for smoke made them very comfortable during the cold season of the year.

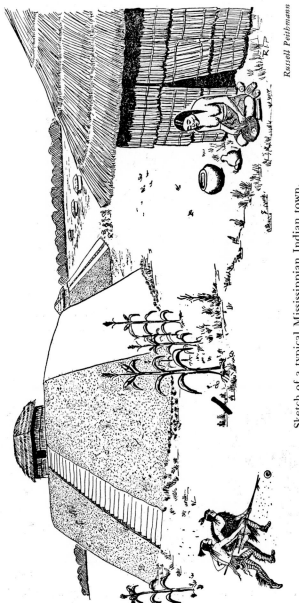

Russell Petithmann

Sketch of a typical Mississippian Indian town.

Human effigy pipe belonging to the Mississpipi culture found at the mouth
of Cave-in Rock, Hardin County, Illinois.

Pottery vessels consisting of bowls and animal-effigy water bottles from
Mississippi sites in southern Illinois.

Irvin M. Peithmann

Typical Mississippi stone effigy pipes: (*left*) human figure bowl on back— Union County, Illinois; (*center*) human figure in squatting position—Pope County, Illinois; (*right*) human figure in squatting position with shield on side—Jackson County, Illinois.

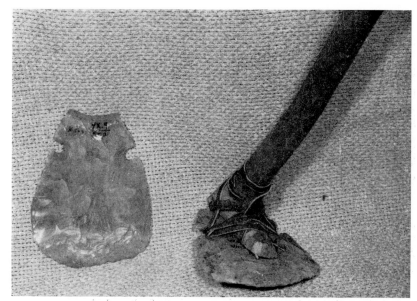

Irvin M. Peithmann

Notched flint hoe and hafting method used by Mississippi Indians.

Typical rock shelter near Indian Creek, southeast of Carbondale, Illinois in Jackson County. (The man in left of picture is the late Dr. John B. Ruyle, Champaign, Illinois.)

University of Chicago

Archaeologists at work at Cove Hollow, Rock Shelter, Jackson County, Illinois.

Outline of house floor, showing location of posts that supported the walls, and a tightly flexed skeleton. Found at Peter's Cave, Jackson County, Illinois, during Southern Illinois University Museum excavations, 1951.

Entrance to Cave-in Rock, overlooking the Ohio River in Hardin County, Illinois.

Irvin M. Peithmann

Tightly bound skeleton found at Peter's Cave during Southern Illinois
University Museum excavations in 1951.

Irvin M. Peithmann

Typical rock shelter in Kerr Bluffs, east of Cobden, in Union County, Illinois.

The Piasa Bird.

Solon Bartnek

Petroglyph of eagle (or other bird) at Peter's Cave, Jackson County,
Illinois.

Reproduction of the legendary *piasa* bird painted on limestone bluffs near the original paintings that were observed by Father Marquette, overlooking the Mississippi River near the present town of Alton, Illinois.

Solon Bartnek

Petroglyphs from Peter's Cave in Jackson County, Illinois, now in Southern Illinois University Museum.

Albert Meyer,
Southern Illinois University Photo Service

Fountain Bluff petroglyphs, Jackson County, Illinois.

Sketch of an eagle, "Thunderbird" made of Repousse sheet copper. This copper effigy was taken from a stone-lined grave in Jackson County, Illinois, many years ago.

Pictograph: original painting of a "buffalo" about two miles north of Simpson, Illinois, in Johnson County, Illinois.

Dancing figures sketched from copper plate found in Union County, Illinois.

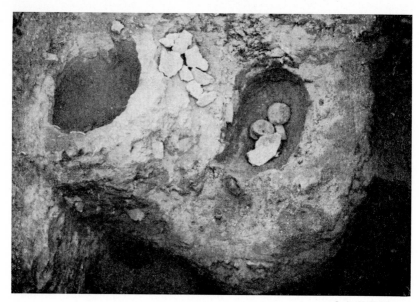

Irvin M. Peithmann

Clay-lined fire basins in midden at Negro Springs site, Gallatin County,
Illinois, excavated by author in 1952.

Irvin M. Peithmann

Large pieces of salt-pan ware showing textile impressions of woven mat-
ting from Negro Springs site in Gallatin County, Illinois.

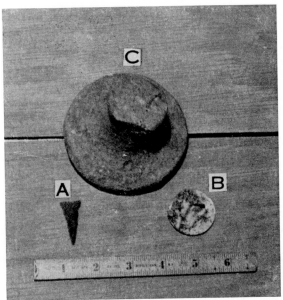

(A) Triangular arrow point, (B) shell disk, (C) pottery trowel for smoothing pottery during manufacture. Found in excavations made by author.

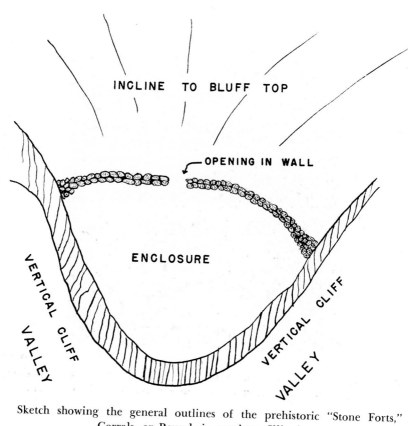

Sketch showing the general outlines of the prehistoric "Stone Forts," Corrals, or Pounds in southern Illinois

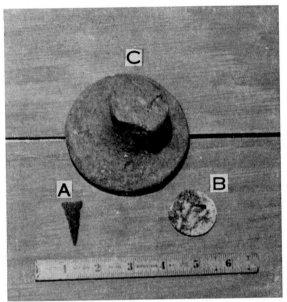

(A) Triangular arrow point, (B) shell disk, (C) pottery trowel for smoothing pottery during manufacture. Found in excavations made by author.

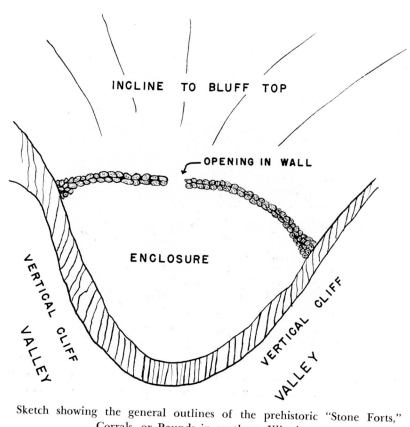

INCLINE TO BLUFF TOP

OPENING IN WALL

ENCLOSURE

VERTICAL CLIFF

VALLEY

VERTICAL CLIFF

VALLEY

Sketch showing the general outlines of the prehistoric "Stone Forts,"
Corrals, or Pounds in southern Illinois

Irvin M. Peithmann

Bison. These animals were a common sight in southern Illinois late in the
seventeenth century.

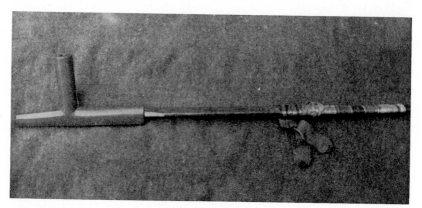

A modern Sioux "peace pipe."

war on the Indians living in Illinois at the time the French were exploring here, had already obtained enough guns to fight a long-range war and defeat the Illinois Indians.

The Indians soon found it was much easier to trade furs for brass and iron kettles than to continue to make their fragile pottery vessels. The white traders also offered them clothing and ready-made trinkets, so that, with the coming of the white man, Indians soon discarded some of their material things.

Important happenings and events were remembered and handed down for about one hundred and fifty years. By that time the stories had either been forgotten or had evolved into legends. This is probably why the Indians found here by the first explorers did not recognize the mounds as the work of some of their predecessors, or have any traditions concerning their origin. The theory that prevailed up to the last half century, that the mound-building Indians were a people separate from the Indians found here by white men, was conceived partly because of this. Village sites, graves, petroglyphs, stone walls, and mounds are evidences of Indian traditions of the past.

Heretofore many persons interested in archaeology have been confused by the often-used term "mound builder." The prehistoric Indians that preceded the Indians found here by the early French explorers did build mounds for different purposes, depending on what Indians built them. Some were built as monuments to the dead that were buried in them, while others were built with flat tops so that houses or temples could be erected on them. Not all the prehistoric Indians built mounds; for example, the first hunters and Indians living during the early Archaic period did not build mounds. They did not have the time, nor had they evolved a philosophy of respect for the dead and of worship of a deity, such as some of the later prehistoric Indians practiced. (See sections on Hopewellian and Mississippian Indians.)

When one sees a mound of earth built by the Indians long ago, one should remember that human labor lies behind these ancient monuments, for they were built of loads of dirt carried in skin baskets on the shoulders or in the arms of the prehistoric Indians. Devotion is perhaps the strongest of human sentiments.

The passions of love, hate, and pride have, for centuries, covered the earth with their monuments.

Traditional customs follow people wherever they go. Many of our traditions date back to old customs. Our civilization is a "transplanted" culture brought from Europe; the pioneers left marks of their traditions, which they brought with them from Europe, when they moved westward from the eastern seacoast. These traditions are noticeable around the old homesteads of the early settlers. The styles of the houses they built, and the selection of the trees, flowers, and shrubbery they planted, are due to traditions they brought with them from the east. When our European ancestors came here directly from Europe, their houses were styled much like the homes they left in their ancestral homeland.

One of the most interesting things in rural life is the preservation of the old traditions. Changes in ways of thinking and acting come slowly. We continue to do things as they were done by our pioneer forefathers one hundred years ago. Many of the old customs have been outmoded in the larger towns and cities; however, in our rural communities, we still do many things in the old traditional way. Old traditions, even in present-day civilization, are hard to break away from. The hanging of a horseshoe over the doorway as an omen of good luck has been an American tradition for many years. However, the use of this symbol today is more or less traditional. Here we have an example of a custom that has continued for many years but has lost its original intent. Further examples of this are wearing of religious emblems, charms or rabbit's feet for good luck. Several generations will live in a community before all the old traditions are discarded. In some respects we still follow the traditions of our ancestors. Probably the strongest of these are traditions in politics and religion. However, our rapidly changing culture during the past fifty years has caused us to discard many of the old traditions our forefathers brought with them.

7. Legends

Great epic poems telling of the deeds of heroes, usually drawn from national traditions, are the heritage of most of the cultures of the world. The Greeks had their *Iliad* and their *Odyssey;* the

English, *Beowulf;* and the Germans, the *Niebelungenlied.*

For many years after the discovery of America by Europeans, little or no thought was given to the origin of the Indians or of their habits, customs, legends, myths and traditions.

Since our country was born and grew to maturity in three hundred years, we have only the loosely connected fragments of its folklore, tales, and legends. It fell to the poet Longfellow to weave some of these together in the "Song of Hiawatha," which has become an epic in American literature. Although there is very little known concerning the legends of the historic tribes who lived in southern Illinois, there are many recorded legends of some of the historic Indian tribes who lived in mid-America. Indian imagination created many folk stories, some the result of rare imagination. Many of these became legends.

One of our legendary personages, especially to our young children, is Santa Claus.

The Algonquin Indians, east of the Mississippi River, believed in a great spirit or power which they knew by the name of Manitou. Every Algonquin man of importance was expected to have a supernatural guardian spirit or totem. In their mythology, thunder and lightning were elevated to the level of gods. The idea was that this deity or spirit took the form of a great bird. To us, this is known as the thunderbird of the Indian legends. The traditional legend of this mythical creature, the thunderbird, is but one simple example of Indian folklore which has survived for hundreds of years among many of the Indian tribes. Today it is symbolized on pottery, beadwork, jewelry, and other handicraft of the historic Indian's culture.

Many tribes of Indians in the United States still believe in the traditional legends, sing songs of legends, portray symbols depicting mythical gods, and wear the tribal costumes in the dances of their forefathers.

The Mississippi River is referred to in the Indian legends as the "Father of Waters." The unwritten history of the Choctaws and Chickasaws identifies the Mississippi River as one of their discoveries in their eastward migration from old Mexico. Their medicine man named it "Misha Siphoni" meaning "beyond the ages—the father of its kind."

A love of legends and mysteries is characteristic of all Indians; many of their legends came about because of this trait. The legends of the Potawatomi show rare beauty and imagination. These Indians believed in two spirits—Kitchemonedo, the good spirit; and Matchemonedo, the evil spirit. Kitchemonedo made the world and all the things in it. He peopled it with beings who looked like men who were perverse, ungrateful, and wicked and never raised their eyes from the ground to thank him for anything. At last the Great Spirit plunged the world into a huge lake and drowned them. He then withdrew the world from the water and made a single man, very handsome, but also sad and lonesome; then, to allay his loneliness, Kitchemonedo took pity on the man and sent him a sister. One night the young man had a dream. When he awoke, he said to his sister, "Five young men will come to your lodge door tonight to visit you. You must not talk to the first four. But with the fifth you may speak and laugh." She acted accordingly. The first to call was Usama (tobacco); being repulsed, he fell down and died. The second was Waupako (pumpkin); the third, Eshkossimin (melon); and the fourth, Kokees (bean); all met the same fate. But when Tasmin (maize) presented himself, she received him kindly. They were immediately married, and from this union the Indians sprang. Tasmin buried the four unsuccessful suitors, and from their graves grew tobacco, melons, pumpkins, and beans.

There are scores of Indian legends, several of which have been cited in other sections. Our civilization is not without its share of legends. An example of how some of the legends of our ancestors came about can be found in the legends in Ireland. We have often heard that there are no snakes in Ireland. Irish folklore found it necessary to account for this fact and popular legend says that St. Patrick drove them out. However, biologists, from their scientific investigations, now know that Ireland was already an island long before England was separated from the continent. It is now known that many animals such as snakes were able to cross from France into England before the sea rose to create the English Channel, but they were not able to reach Ireland, since Ireland was already surrounded by water.

8. Magic

Magic, too, often plays a part in the culture of primitive peoples. In their attempt to protect themselves from misfortune and the forces of nature, men through the ages have adopted many curious practices. Centuries ago the Norseman designed the prows of their viking ships with figureheads to resemble dragons or serpents to terrorize the enemy and drive away his protecting spirit. The Indians of many different tribes painted and decorated their bodies to look hideous to the enemy when they went to war.

Every religion has its magic, and what is commonly called "practicing a religion" is practicing its magic. Many of the Christian ceremonies in our social life, such as weddings, funerals, forms of pageantry, and certain interpretive dances, had their beginnings among our early European ancestors.

Most Indians would not think of going to war without having participated in the proper dances beforehand. We know that the function of the war dance was to build up the morale of the war party. The purpose of this magic was to get up enough courage to attack the enemy.

C. Remains of the Indian Cultures

1. Flint Industry

One of the most valuable discoveries of man in his long struggle for existence was the fact that flint could be made into hunting and farming tools. Most of the flint tools such as spearheads, knives, scrapers, chisels, and hoes made and used by the different Indian cultures that lived in southern Illinois, had as their origin the raw material taken by the Indians from the flint deposits of Union County.

Apparently southern Illinois has always been famous for its mining industry. Today the area is noted for its coal, limestone, clays, fluorspar, and other minerals. In prehistoric Indian times, salt and flint were in the spotlight of demand. Just as coal, fluorspar, and clays are today shipped from the area to adjacent states, so in prehistoric times salt and semi-processed flint, as well as manufactured flint tools, moved out of the region to distant places.

There is ample evidence to indicate that the flint quarries

of southern Illinois, especially those in the present political area of Union County, were not only large producers, but also that the material was of excellent quality. There are three areas in Union County where the prehistoric Indians obtained flint. The chert flint at each of these places is in marked contrast to the others, and the quarrying methods used by the different Indian cultures varied to some extent at each place. Different types of coal and clays can be identified by chemical composition, whereas varieties of flint can be identified by color characteristics.

The flint deposits in Union County were some of the first natural resources used by the first Indians when they came to live in southern Illinois. It is known that the Indians found and used the flint deposits at a very early time, because the hunting tools of the Archaic, the Woodland, and the Hopewellian people living in the area at different times were made for the most part from flint deposits southwest of Cobden, Illinois.

In this area, scattered in the creek beds, are found round, ball-like nodules, covered with a buff-colored covering or bark— due to aging—ranging from two to eight inches in diameter. When broken open, the nodules or balls show alternate rings of blue-black "hornstone" flint. The Indians obtained these ball-like nodules probably by gathering them up and taking them to their camps, or by breaking them up into smaller pieces nearby and selecting the choice pieces of flint to be made later into flint hunting tools.

Ages ago, when the ice-choked glacial waters from the melting ice fields to the north were cutting out the valleys in the Shawnee hills south of Carbondale, they left evidence in the form of water-deposited ball-shaped stones in the gravel fills in the upper Clear Creek Valley in Union County. The wearing action of this fast-moving water through these flood-choked valleys loosened these ball-like stones from a limestone formation and carried them to this valley, where they were deposited in with other water-worn sandstone pebbles. Many of the larger ones were chipped and broken by the action of the fast-moving water as they were pushed along, exposing the high-grade hornstone flint inside them. Clear Creek came into existence at a later time, exposing these glacial water-deposited flint balls.

Many centuries later, probably around ten thousand years ago, when the early Archaic Indian hunters first moved into southern Illinois, they found these flint balls; in them they saw great possibilities as much-needed material for making hunting tools, such as flint spearheads, scrapers, and knives. Through the centuries, Indians came from far and near to dig and pick up in the creek bed the choicest of these flint balls.

Evidence of their former workshops can still be seen on the terraces near the creek and adjacent hills, close to the deposits. Tons of these broken balls litter the fields in the area, and in addition there are thousands of flint chips, an occasional flint spearhead, or knife—mute evidence that the first inhabitants of southern Illinois utilized its natural resources many thousands of years ago.

In many of the prehistoric Indian towns, villages, and camp sites in southern Illinois are to be found pieces of flint that, at one time, were chipped from the flint balls of Union County.

In the same general area, on a series of ridges, there are other flint deposits of semitransparent flint, locally called novaculite. This flint is of many colors and varying shades of purple, pink, tan, buff, cream and white.

Methods Used in Quarrying Flint

The quarrying or mining by the Indians on these ridges was more or less a "groundhog" type of mining—that is, holes were dug or "burrowed" into the sides of the ridges without always removing the overburden of earth covering the flint deposit. Much of the raw material from this quarry site was carried away and converted into hunting tools, such as spearheads, knives, and scrapers, by the Archaic, the Woodland, and the Hopewellian people, who preceded the Mississippi people by many centuries. The Mississippi people knew of and used materials from this flint deposit, even to the extent of setting up workshops near Clear Creek.

Workshops of Mississippi Indians Near Clear Creek

Several workshops or manufacturing places used by these Indians exist near Clear Creek. One of these is located by a large spring near the north end of the ridge where the main deposit is located. An Indian trail is still visible on this ridge leading from the flint workshop to the flint deposit. This flint factory was on a smaller scale than the ones near the Mill Creek quarry farther south. The farming tools, such as spades and hoes, that have been found here are of the same shape and size as those from the Mill Creek workshop site; however, they are fewer in number compared to those that have been found that were made from Mill Creek flint. The Clear Creek flint factory was used by the Mississippi Indians in about the same way as the ones they operated near the Mill Creek quarry.

This is in contrast to the way some of the first hunting people, at an earlier time, worked at this quarry site. It appears that they came and selected smaller pieces of flint and carried them away, probably in skin bags, to their villages, where they worked up the material into hunting tools in their leisure time. There is no reason to believe that the early Archaic and later Woodland hunting people worked here on a day-to-day basis; it seems that they came only to obtain flint as the need arose.

Location of Mill Creek Flint Quarries

About eight miles south of Jonesboro (Union County) and several miles south and west of the present village of Mill Creek, there is a series of high ridges or hills underlain with a strata of flatish, nodular, buff-and-tan-colored flint. On this timber-covered ridge and extending over a large area there is evidence of a prehistoric Indian flint industry. The numerous pits and trenches the Indians dug in the ground to get to the flint strata under the surface of the ground appear to the present-day visitor about the same as to the last Indian worker who left them possibly four or five hundred years ago.

Many of the excavations made in prehistoric Indian times are still ten or more feet deep and ten to twenty feet across, with a ridge of dirt surrounding these depressions. Investigations made years ago revealed that some of the excavations had originally been forty or more feet deep. Because of their exposed position, they have filled in to their present depth. The early settlers in the area referred to them as the "Indian diggings."

Most, if not all, of the operations in obtaining flint at the Mill Creek quarry and other small ones on adjacent ridges in the vicinity were done by the farming Mississippi people who were still living in southern Illinois several centuries before the first white man arrived.

The Mill Creek flint deposits were not used to any extent by the early hunting cultures because this material was not suited for the making of such hunting tools as spearheads. Because of the impurities found in it, it did not respond to the pressure flaking used in making these weapons. However, it was wonderful material to work with when the percussion method was used in chipping the larger farming implements, such as notched hoes and spades.

Method of Manufacture

The flint was removed from the quarry in large enough pieces or slabs to make the manufacturing or chipping into spades and hoes an easy process. After these slabs were dug from the ground, the best ones were carefully selected and blocked out with hammerstones. In this rough shape or "blank" form they were carried to a nearby workshop to be finished. Some probably were taken directly from the quarry to the towns and villages to be finished into farming implements and other tools. The Indians also set up workshops adjacent to the quarries they worked, partly because of the size of the raw flint material it took to make a finished hoe or spade. It was easier to finish the product in the vicinity and then take it away. At best, one person could not carry more than a dozen flint hoes or spades, since the size of these implements ranged anywhere from four to six inches in width and eight to sixteen inches in length.

Flint-manufacturing Site and Water Factor

There is evidence that only a few of the Indians came to make flint farming tools near the quarry site. It was not practical for a group of workers who would probably have to bring along their families to live on these high ridges where water was not available for drinking.

The Indians were the first people living here to recognize

the importance of a good water supply; the early pioneer always located near springs or streams to assure an available water supply for his needs. Today the modern industrialist seeks an adequate water supply before building or locating factories in an area, just as the Indians who came to live near the flint quarries in Union County found it easier to bring the flint they dug on the ridges to a water supply rather than take the water to the quarry site.

Mill Creek Flint Factory

About two and one half miles southeast of the Mill Creek quarry site, and within the perimeter of other like deposits, is the site of a large flint tool manufacturing center. Here, near a large spring on a low ridge lying on the north side of Mill Creek, the Indians set up their workshop or flint factory. A casual observer who might visit the site would not help but notice the large amount of flint chips on the ground; broken hoes and spades in every stage of manufacture; large flat flint nodules; and large pieces of flint as they were brought from the quarry. This layer of flint chippings extends downward into the ground for several feet. All this evidence points to the fact that here was the center of a large flint industry. It was probably the more skilled workers who did most of the chipping and finishing of these flint farming tools, while others dug the flint from the quarry and carried it to the workshop, always keeping an available supply of raw materials on hand. Still others were probably busy hunting and farming small patches of corn nearby to assure a good food supply.

Trading and Transportation of Flint and Flint Products

Flint farming implements made of this Mill Creek flint have been found on Indian village sites many miles away. Indians coming from distant places probably traded food, such as wild game they hunted on the way, for tools the Indian flint workers were making at this factory.

The finding of flint chisels, hoes, and spades made of Mill Creek flint at distant Indian villages raises a question: How did these Indians transport the bulky flint—as raw material or finished implements?

Even though these quarries and workshops were not far removed from streams that now flow intermittently and dry up in summer, it is doubtful whether the streams were of much value to the Indians in transporting flint to their villages in dugout boats. It is more likely that flint was transported on the backs of Indians who made trips to the flint quarries for raw materials or to the flint factory to trade and barter for finished products from the Indians. Probably a part of the trip home was made by water, because they could walk overland from the Mississippi River, a distance of not over ten miles, and stop at the large Indian village on Clear Creek, west of the quarry and workshop site, on their journey to and from the site, picking up provision at each stop.

It would be interesting to know the laws and customs which protected these places. Through legend we know there were places that were neutral ground, such as the pipestone quarry in Minnesota, where Indians went without fear of attack.[8]

There are no such legends or traditions concerning the use historic Indians made of these flint quarries in Union County. For many years farmers all over southern Illinois have found in their fields flint implements and hunting tools that were made from the flint the Indians obtained in Union County and were left by the Archaic, the Woodland, the Hopewellian, and the Mississippian Indians.

Methods of Chipping Flint

There are many people who have many different ideas about how the Indians made their flint spearheads and implements. Some still believe that by heating a piece of flint and by putting small drops of water on it, flakes will be chipped off, leaving a finished spearhead or knife. It was not that simple for the Indians, who were masters in the field of rock cleavage. They seem to have used two methods to chip flint tools: the percussion method and the pressure method.

PERCUSSION METHOD—The percussion method of chipping was performed by using a hammerstone (a uniformly shaped stone generally of hard quartzite or granite materials), and sometimes a piece of flint, that could be held easily in the hand. Sometimes

---

[8]According to tradition, the pipestone quarry in Minnesota was neutral ground where tribal enmities were put aside. The story of this pipestone quarry was popularized in Longfellow's "Song of Hiawatha."

these stones were slightly pitted on each side to enable the user to get a better grip, and quite often they became worn round like a ball from the continuous use to which they were subjected in pecking the flint in order to strike off the desired flakes from the flint tool or implement which the Indian happened to be making. This is the way by which much of the large ball flint was reduced to disks and knives, leaving a small flint core, which was then discarded. This technique was used by the Hopewellian Indians.

Pressure Method—The pressure method was performed by placing a blunt-pointed bone tool at an angle against the edge of the flint to be made into a spearhead or knife and by applying enough pressure to throw off small flakes. By controlling the chipping in this manner, a skilled flint worker was able to turn out symmetrical spearheads and other flint implements. Most of the flint used was carefully selected flawless material.

2. Salt Industry

Half Moon Lick

About a mile south of the present town of Equality (Gallatin County) there is a large depression in the ground about fifteen feet deep. This depression lies on the northwest side of the Saline River and has been referred to as "the Great Salt Lick." According to tradition, game animals such as bison, elk, and deer came in prehistoric Indian times and "licked out" this semicircular depression.

A careful observation of this depression suggests that it was at one time the original channel of the Saline River, the river later changing its course. The idea that the depression was made by a former river channel does not, however, discount the fact that it was used as a lick by animals in Indian times. There are trail-like depressions leading into this lick that may well have been made by bison and other animals coming to lick the salty earth.

At present the site is covered with a heavy growth of timber; in prehistoric times it was probably an alluvial swamp. The depression or lick is about two hundred yards wide and the curve extends for a length of about two hundred and fifty yards. Because of its shape it is known locally as Half Moon Lick, although it more nearly resembles a horseshoe.

It is interesting to note that remains of mammoths have been found in recent years during dredging and drainage operations in the swampland in the area. Whether these animals made use of the salty earth would be purely conjecture.

There is good reason to believe, however, that at this early time these salt springs were in existence. A rock fault in the area caused or formed the springs, the water coming to the surface through this fault from a salt deposit deep in the rock strata. This fault can still be seen near the salt springs and in the bed of the Saline River during dry seasons. The salt licks on the Saline River became the greatest in the United States and were highly valued by the Indians.

The Salt Springs

Colonial development: Southeast of Equality—about three miles—and within a few yards of the south side of the Saline River, there is a natural-flowing salt spring called, locally, "Negro Springs." It gets its name from the fact that white men brought slave labor here to work while Illinois was still a territory and for some time after it became a state in the year 1818.

Large iron kettles were brought down the Ohio River from the east and were used to boil or evaporate the brine from this spring. A good grade of salt was still a rare article in colonial times; and the salt made from this spring and others in the area was of very good quality. The government, realizing the importance of the area as a source of a continuous salt supply, set aside several hundred acres in the area as a government reservation and leased it to individuals who drilled many wells in the nearby region, making it at that time the greatest producer of salt in the United States.

The quest for salt and its use had been one of the great life lines of history; prehistoric as well as historic people valued it for its preservative and seasoning values.

Prehistoric Salt Industry

Just as the salt springs and wells were important to white men during the colonial period and later development of our country, they were also important to the earlier Indians.

At the salt springs there is evidence of a prehistoric Indian salt industry and pottery-manufacturing center. An area of about thirty acres around this spring is littered with broken saltpan vessels, and over the years many other objects of Indian origin have been found. This site has been known to archaeologists for many years, but little or no investigations had been made until the author investigated the site late in 1952. From the pieces of pottery found and the profusion of broken salt-pan ware, it has been established that the Mississippian Indians lived here late in prehistoric times.

In the fall of 1952 the author made some preliminary investigations around this spring, among them the digging of several test pits to determine the depth of the midden deposit and to check the potsherds for evidence of Indian cultures other than those left by the Mississippi people. One of these test pits was carried down four feet to the clay sub-floor base—the original ground level before the Indians came to live or camp here. Near the bottom of this pit many pieces of pottery were found belonging to the Woodland people, who lived here before the Mississippi people came. Whether these earlier Woodland people came to get salt or whether this was a good camping place cannot be determined by present evidence. However, it is possible that these earlier people came and obtained salt formed at the spring by natural evaporation. In other words, they collected salt that had crusted on the ground or on stones near the spring but they did not manufacture it.

From the study of the material found in the test pits (broken salt pans, pottery vessels, and pottery trowels used in smoothing the vessels when made) and the depth of the midden, it is concluded that this site was used for several centuries by the Mississippi people as a salt-making center. Numerous clay-lined fire basins, which may have been used in connection with drying salt or for other unknown purpose, were found in several of the test pits. Although an early writer referred to the Indians who made salt here as "salt boilers,"[9] there is no positive evidence that fire was used under these pottery vats to evaporate the water.

---

[9]Wm. N. Moyer, "The Seven Wonders of Egypt," *Journal of the Illinois State Historical Society*, XXVII, p. 190.

Many years ago a few entire salt pans were found here. These shallow pans were from three to four feet in diameter and were made of clay mixed with pounded or crushed mussel shell. However, judging from the evidence of the broken evaporating vessels, the breakage must have been great.

Method of Manufacture and Use of Salt Pans: The Indians manufactured salt pans, it seems, as they were needed. Almost all the broken pieces show textile impressions or the imprint of loosely woven or plaited fiber netted on the underside. This netting or fiber was probably made from the inner parts of bark or grasses, woven somewhat like the netting used in our fish nets, and was probably used to reinforce the vessels to keep them from cracking while the wet clay was drying. This netting probably was removed after the vessel had hardened from drying, and later the vessel was fired over a slow fire to harden it still further.

Method Used to Obtain Salt: These shallow pans or vessels were nothing more than evaporating vats, which were filled with brine and set out in the sun. When the water had evaporated, the salt that had crusted in the vessels was scraped up and put in other pottery vessels or skin bags, then the process repeated. If this industry was seasonal, most of the salt-making probably took place during the hot summer months when condensation would be at its best.

The Saline River, so called because of the brine it carries, is still navigable for small boats except during the dry periods of the year. Probably about five hundred years ago, when this prehistoric industry was at its peak, the river stage was more stable than it is now and the site could be reached by dugout boats most of the year. It is quite possible that Indians coming to trade for salt from distant places made use of water travel as well as trails overland.

The Mississippi people were also farmers and probably did some farming nearby. If the site was occupied over a long period of time (as the depth of midden deposits seems to suggest), the game attracted to the area to lick salt may have solved, in part, the food problem. An extensive cemetery on the bluff suggests that at one time quite a village existed around the spring and near the river. The cemetery has been destroyed by treasure hunters;

only scattered slabs of stone that had lined some of the graves are left. A number of pottery pipes were found in these graves years ago. An examination of all the evidence points to the fact that the Mississippi people made salt here for many years. One may ask, "Did the Indians who left all the material evidence have unlimited control over the salt-making for a long period of time?" It appears that they did. The broken salt pans examined are of about the same texture and general shape, leaving no ceramic evidence that any people other than the Mississippians had evaporated salt here. They were the "Morton Salt people" of their day. However, evidence has recently been found that earlier Woodland people had lived near the spring before the coming of the Mississippi people.[10]

Local Tradition: There is a local tradition that has lasted many years in the form of a legend concerning a Piankashaw chief who, on hearing of salt springs in Illinois, had a band of his hardiest braves cross the Ohio and Wabash rivers. Here in southern Illinois they found salt springs which they called the Great Salt Springs, and the salt lick. Legend does not say where these Indians had been living, only that they were of the Algonquin family and crossed the Ohio and Wabash rivers, which would place them in Indiana or Kentucky. The Piankashaw chief and his tribe settled near the springs and evaporated the highly prized salt, which they bartered to other Indians for flint tools, clothing, food, and handiwork. Later this chief traded with the white man in the same manner, finally selling the rights of the tribe to two men, Mr. Temple and Mr. Broughton. The town Broughton, in Hamilton County, was named after the latter.

3. "Stone Forts," Corrals, or Pounds

One of the unique prehistoric phenomena of southern Illinois are the ruins of stone walls which have traditionally been known as "stone forts." They appear in a roughly east-west alignment across the hill country and appear to form a broken chain between the Ohio and Mississippi rivers. These ruins have similar

---

[10]Peithmann, Irvin, "A preliminary report on salt-making and pottery manufacture at a prehistoric site in Gallatin County, Illinois," *Journal of Illinois State Archaeological Society*, Vol. III, No. 3, September, 1953.

geographic site characteristics. They are generally located on bluffs, which are often finger-like promontories of land with steep cliffs on three sides and a gradual incline on the fourth. It was across inclines leading to the top of the bluff that these stone walls were most generally located. Hence, the theory of a pound or game trap has been advanced.

Many of the walls have long been torn down and removed for building purposes. Early settlers, in most instances, removed the better, slablike stones for building foundations, leaving only the rubble. These early white pioneers saw the walls and thought of them in terms of their own experiences, particularly from the standpoint of defense against the Indians. Though they called them stone forts, these sites would have been very poor places to carry on prolonged fights. If a small band took refuge behind the wall, they might be pushed over the cliff by a larger attacking force. Or a larger force could lay siege to the place, and the band would be cut off from both food and water and soon would starve to death. Although they called them "forts," many people did not accept such a theory, and speculation continued.

Archaeologists believe that, particularly in Ohio, the Hopewellian Indians probably were responsible for some of the walls, but the identity of the builders in southern Illinois is not known. These walls represent a major accomplishment for a people who had only primitive digging implements and methods of carrying stone. These unknown builders piled rock completely across summits, leaving inside enclosures sometimes as large as fifty acres (depending upon the size of the bluff).

Archaeological Investigations

No archaeological investigations have been undertaken in regard to these stone walls, the ancient works of man. No artifacts, except a few archaic spear points, have been found in quantity near these walls to identify them with any particular culture. No evidence of large prehistoric Indian villages has been found near any of these sites. There is, however, much evidence of Archaic and Woodland camping places near the bluffs on which these stone ruins are located. There have been theories advanced for almost every possible use of these walls. The enclosed bluffs may have been stockaded or palisaded by upright posts for use as a fort, but there is no evidence bearing out this theory. They may have been used to some extent for clan or tribal rituals. The theory that they were used as game traps in hunting, however, seems to be the most widely supported idea. Deer and elk may have been impounded or driven off the cliff and killed by the Indians for their winter supply of meat.

Early settlers found a number of gaps in ravines between bluffs near the center of Hardin County closed by high rock walls. Some thought that they were for the purpose of trapping deer. Since these canyons were narrow and came to a dead end, an animal would not have had a chance to escape the hunter.

A local tradition is that these stone-walled enclosures may have been bison pounds, or places where bison were driven over the cliff to be slaughtered by Indians. No archaeological evidence of bison remains has been found in the village refuse or midden deposits in the former living places of the early Indian hunting people in this area; however, evidence points to the fact that historic plains Indians in the west drove bison over bluffs or high precipices to slaughter them. Bison remains have been "reported" to have come from some of the Indian sites that were in existence several centuries prior to the coming of white men to this area. Several bison horns were found during excavations by the Illinois State Museum (1952) at the historic Kaskaskia Indian site in Randolph County. This site dates from the year 1700 and substantiates the early records of the French that there were bison in this area in the latter part of the seventeenth and the early eighteenth centuries.

If these stone-walled enclosures were used as pounds or slaughtering places for bison, no evidence has been found to support it. W. N. Moyer, of Mounds City, Illinois, gives the location and description of seven of these walls.[11] Since then, although there have been stories about several other walls, only two more have been reported and mapped. Following is a description of these walls and some of the local traditions concerning the nine walls that have been found.

Giant City Park: Within the environs of Giant City Park,

---

[11]Moyer, *op. cit.*, p. 193.

across a seventy-foot bluff, lies the ruin of a 285-foot stone wall. According to local tradition, the wall was originally six feet high and six feet thick, made of stones laid apparently without mortar. About 125 feet from the west end was a gateway or opening in the wall. Though part of the wall has been "restored," most of it is still in ruins.

Stonefort: The present town of Stonefort, Illinois (Saline County), received its name from a nearby ancient wall called "Old Stone Fort." This "fort" is on a sandstone bluff which rises more than 100 feet above Little Saline Creek, which flows past its base. Though the wall was torn down long ago and very little of it remains to be seen, it appears originally to have been a 300-foot oval-shaped wall enclosing about two acres of the bluff top. Historical tradition reports that when government surveyors noted the presence of this wall in about 1809, it was then six feet high and six feet wide, with the enclosed area overgrown with timber.

Draper's Bluff: Draper's Bluff is a 300-foot sandstone escarpment on the east side of Lick Creek Valley (Johnson and Union counties). The south point of the bluff turns due east for about 1000 feet into Johnson County, forming a ridge about 400 feet wide. Across the center of this ridge lie the traces of a stone wall, showing it to have been built across the entire width of the ridge. Early settlers say it was six feet high by as many feet thick, and enclosed about ten acres of land.

Indian Kitchen: Water Lane Pound, or Indian Kitchen, in Pope County, is one of the least-known bluffs where there is still a portion of the original stone wall intact. Lusk Creek forms a U with parallel, vertical bluffs on each side. The cut in the U is about 150 feet high, 190 feet wide, and 700 feet long. A stone wall built across the mouth of the U encloses a two and one-half-acre plot of ground. Moyer[12] states that a small section of the original wall was intact about twenty years ago. On the south side of the bluff is a rock shelter called Indian Kitchen in which have been found pieces of flint and pottery of Indian design.

War Bluff: This bluff is one at the east end of a flat ridge or

---

[12]*Ibid.*, p. 187.

plateau near the town of Raum, Illinois (Pope County). This ridge slopes gently toward the east end, where it forms an abruptly vertical, semicircular cliff about 300 feet high. At the point where the slope narrows and rises rather steeply, there are the remains of a stone wall extending fifty feet across the cliff, enclosing an area of two or more acres of parklike timbered land. This enclosure has the outward appearance of either a fortification or a pound. On the lower slope, about four or five rods in front of the stone wall, and lying at an oblique angle to the first wall, is the ruin of another stone wall. This tumble-down wall is about 300 feet long and extends across the bluff from cliff to cliff. There are many local stories which are associated with this bluff. They concern Indian fights and sieges. The stories of skirmishes white men had with the Indians here are without foundation or fact, yet the title War Bluff remains.

The Pounds: Near the south line of Gallatin County is a walled bluff, known for 150 years as the Pounds, which is now part of the Shawnee National Forest. The bluff has an average height of about 150 feet and is approached from the southeast by a narrow ridge presenting only a twenty-foot climb. At this point lie the ruins of a stone barricade extending across the 150-yard area of the ridge. Inside the stone wall, on top of the bluff, are about fifty acres of land, forty of which were at one time in cultivation but have since been reforested. In the rock marginal area around the top, which has never been farmed, old rock cairns (piles of stones), which apparently were put there by early settlers in land-clearing operations, may be seen. This enclosure is the largest of any found in southern Illinois, and appears to be what its name suggests, a pound or corral in which animals were killed. Traditionally, it has been known as a pound since white men first settled the area.

Cornish Bluff Fort: Cornish Bluff, a few miles from Reynoldsburg, Illinois (Johnson County), is a semicircular bluff facing south, on the top of which there was at one time a stone wall. This wall is similar to the others described, differing only in the fact that it has a semicircular shape. Beginning at the west side of the bluff the wall outline trends east for thirty rods, then turns at a 45° angle toward the southeast for another thirty rods. Since all the land on top has been in cultivation for many years, a large portion of the old wall has been piled up by farmers. The view from this bluff top is magnificent, commanding an area of many miles.

Trigg Stone Fort: Trigg Stone Fort is a recently discovered stone wall on a high hill in Johnson County. Like many of the other walls, it has been practically destroyed. L. O. Trigg reported that early farmers encouraged settlers to remove stones and over 100 loads were removed for foundations and other needs of early pioneers. Near this wall is a so-called "smoke tower," supposedly built by the Indians for signalling purposes. This is probably nothing more than a pile of stones that may even have been made by early settlers during clearing operations.

Thomas Stone Fort: This fort is at another location which has been recently brought to the attention of archaeologists. The site is about three miles east of Cobden (Union County). An early settler knew of the stone ruin, but it could not be located again until 1930 when it was found by Joe and Charles Thomas of Cobden.

Until a time period is established for these stone walls, it will be difficult to assign them to any particular prehistoric Indian cultural group. However, exploration and excavation of these sites may help in solving the mystery of these stone walls.

4. Rock Shelters

In the Shawnee Hills of southern Illinois there are many high cliffs. These almost vertical, rocky slopes are composed of alternate layers of sedimentary sandstone rock which have been worn away by weathering. Streams that at one time existed near the base of these cliffs have undercut in places and left an overhanging ledge. These places are known as rock shelters. In nearly every case there was at one time a permanent- or intermittent-flowing spring or stream nearby which offered a water supply. These shelters, which offered protection or cover from the elements for prehistoric and historic Indians, early travelers and settlers, now offer shelter to the livestock of the present-day farmers in the area.

Archaeological Evidence Found

Archaeological evidence recovered in some of the shelters that have been partly excavated has furnished proof that rock shelters were lived in and used extensively over a period of many centuries. From the time when the first Indian hunters came into this area, the shelters had been inhabited by a succession of Indian peoples. The dirt floor or fill, called midden by archaeologists, was found in some of these shelters to be many feet thick and extending down to bedrock. In this fill have been recovered many artifacts left by the Indians who lived there at different times. Most of the material recovered is an accumulation of bits of discarded animal bones, flint projectile points, flint scrapers, knives, bone awls, potsherds (pieces of broken pottery vessels), and burnt stones used around fireplaces.

Our modern towns have their refuse dumps some distance from town. It will be here that the archaeologist of the future will search for clues of our civilization. During Indian times the refuse accumulated on the spot where they lived and built up layer on layer as the years passed.

The ground on which an Indian village once existed, or the dirt floor of a rock shelter, varies in the depth of the deposit, or midden, in which the remains are found according to the length of time the site was inhabited. Many of these sites, whether they were living places out in the open (camp sites) or rock shelters, because of their favorable location, were inhabited by different Indian cultures over a period of many centuries. This caused an overlapping of cultural materials left by the Indians. The ground was built up by the accumulation of things left by one Indian group and added to by things left by succeeding Indian groups. Archaeologists refer to this arrangement and succession of strata as stratigraphy. Sometimes the Indians buried their dead in the dirt floor of the shelter. Later, other Indians came to live there, unaware of its previous use, and also buried some of their dead. In some of the shelters the inhabitants left carvings and paintings on the wall.[13]

The prehistoric Indians probably used these shelters because they were located in hidden, out-of-the-way places, and because they were a natural protection against the elements. They moved

---

[13]See "Pictographs and Petroglyphs," p. 76.

into these "ready-made" homes furnished by nature, thereby saving the time and labor required to construct a crude shelter or house elsewhere. What more could a primitive Indian ask for? Here he could move in with his family and call it a home, and when he left them to hunt for food, he had some assurance that his family would have protection from the weather and the wild animals he was hunting for food and clothing.

Location of Shelters

Some of the better-known rock shelters in southern Illinois are Cove Hollow, east of Pomona (Jackson County) ; Hawk Cave, at Ferne Clyffe State Park (Johnson County) ; Cave-in-Rock (Hardin County) ; the large shelter east of Cobden (Union County) ; the large shelter in Clarida Hollow (Pope County) ; Peter's Cave, near Kincaid Creek, about ten miles northwest of Murphysboro (Jackson County) ; the Indian Creek shelter southeast of Carbondale; and the Chalk Bluff shelter, near the Big Muddy River, southwest of Murphysboro (both in Jackson County). There are many more shelters scattered over the area that have not been mentioned or investigated.

Many of the Indian villages and camp sites have been farmed over for years and are no longer visible. However, the rock shelters remain as tangible evidence of the first homes of man in southern Illinois.

5. Indian Trails

The principal Indian trails were beaten deep into the earth for generations by the passing of hundreds of moccasined feet. Many of these trails were the shortest and the best routes; in many cases they were the forerunners of routes for modern travel. Many Indian footpaths, with the coming of the pioneers, were widened into wagon roads, many becoming at a later time the modern paved highways of the present day. One of these former Indian trails in Illinois became one of the crossroads of modern-day travel in America. This trail is now a part of the U. S. Highway 50 between East St. Louis, Illinois, and Vincennes, Indiana.

These old trails that crisscrossed the country were in some respects like our network of roads, because they led to distant places and in all directions. Today these old trails (except on ridges in timbered sections) are no longer in existence, because they were destroyed when farms were laid out and plowed.

The old Indian trail that led north from Shawneetown to Vincennes probably is the one that passed to the south of the historic Piankashaw village site northwest of Albion in Edwards County. This trail crossed Edwards Couny in a southwest-northeast direction to Bone Gap and then ran northward, joining the Cahokia-Vincennes trail near the Embarrass River, southeast of Lawrenceville. Other trails crossed southern Illinois from Kaskaskia to Shawneetown and from Kashaskia to Vincennes.

The Indian custom was to travel single file, leaving a narrow, well-defined trail to their favorite meeting places. Their trails led from village to village, or to shallow places in streams and rivers where the Indians crossed over by wading. These trails were often those used by deer and other animals; pioneers often referred to them as "buffalo traces." In the hill country the Indians, when possible, followed the ridges and high ground. This was an advantage, since the high ground was dry. From these high places they could observe the landscape for game and possible enemies.

The Indian was a master woodsman who excelled in stalking game along these trails.

In Union County some of these old trails may still be seen on the ridges in the vicinity of the old flint quarries and workshops. They still appear about the same as when the Indians used them—narrow and well defined.

In Hardin County, on a ridge near the Saline River, a section of an old trail can still be traced. Trees have now grown up in the trail, while in places where it became deeply worn another path was made close by, paralleling the original trail.

Many other trails can still be traced on the wooded ridges of Hardin, Pope, Union, Jackson, Johnson and Gallatin counties and in surrounding areas in southern Illinois.

6. Indian Art: Pictographs and Petroglyphs

Before white men came, prehistoric Indian artists were leaving their art carved and painted on the walls of rock shelters and on cliff walls in the Shawnee Hills of southern Illinois. Scattered over this area there were, at one time, many pictographs. These pictographs, which were monochromatic pictures intended to express ideas, were usually colored a faded brown to red by using a mixture of powdered iron oxide and red and yellow ocher mixed with animal grease, which penetrated the wall on which they were painted and preserved the design. In addition to pictographs, the Indians left pictures which were carved and pecked in stone by using a piece of flint or hard stone. These are known as petroglyphs.

The first reference to the finding of pictographs was made by Father Marquette on his voyage down the Mississippi River in the year 1673. Near the present-day city of Alton he found a picture of two hideous monsters called *piasa* ("man-eating") birds on an eighty-foot-high river bluff.

There are two Indian legends as to who placed these hideous creatures there and why they did so. A Miami tradition states that many years before the coming of white man, two monsters with wings like huge eagles, alligator claws, and horrible voices—one sounding like a roaring bull and the other like a screaming panther—lived in the cave of the Piasa Bluff. During a battle in which the Miami were beating the Michigamea, these two birds swooped down with horrible screams and each carried away a Miami chieftain, frightening the Miami Indians so badly that they fled beyond the Wabash.

Another story, according to Illinois tradition, tells that such a bird killed or carried off papooses, squaws, and Indian braves. The brave Indian chief went out to decoy the monster from its cave so his warriors could kill it. Legend claims the plan worked without harming the chief, and this picture was painted in memory of the event. The picture was of the piasa bird and was blasted away many years ago, but a replica has been painted in its place.

Petroglyphs are commonly found on standstone outcroppings, on rock hill sides, on large slabs in creek beds, and in rock shelters. However, because of deterioration through weathering, very few petroglyphs remain except in protected places on rock shelter walls.

For the most part the motifs discovered in southern Illinois follow a consistent pattern and are found in groupings in different parts of the area. The equal-arm cross in a circle and the weeping-eye symbol appear to be "trade marks," and are often found along with figures of birds, lizards, snakes, spiders, mammals, human feet and hands, and the human form. Some of these animal figures may have been indicative of the clan or totem of the artist who made them. The concentric rings, the swastika inside a circle, and the circle or sun symbol are designs that seem to have been symbols of Indian mythology or religion.

Designs similar to those in pictographs and petroglyphs have been found on their ornaments. Years ago an incised copper plate depicting a pair of dancing men armed with short ceremonial axes was found in a stone-lined grave on the Mississippi River bluff southwest of Jonesboro in Union County. Shell gorgets with a similar design have been found in the area in Indian graves belonging to the Mississippi cultural pattern. Some of these symbols are found in the art traditions of present-day Indians. Two of these symbols still in use are the thunderbird and the swastika. This suggests that some of the figures found on cliff walls in this area may have been totems used in tribal rituals which have been handed down to present-day tribes.

Symbolism is a part of our Christian religion and is found in all religions practiced throughout the world. One of the most striking peculiarities of certain tribes of Indians of the Northwest coast is their belief in totems, which they symbolize by means of a totem pole. They were family coats of arms depicting the history and legends of a household. These poles are grotesquely carved and gaudily painted with a series of totemic symbols illustrating a belief in a kinship between themselves and the created world, and as such are the totem, or badge, of an individual Indian, or of his family, or of his tribe. It is an example of primitive Indian art and religion, embracing genealogy, myth, charms, evil spirits, legends and witchcraft. These totems, or symbols, are chosen for a reason—either from some past benefits derived from them or from some association of the totem with their lives; they are therefore regarded with a superstitious and almost sacred reverence, but not idolatory.

The symbols carved on the totems represent relationships of

clans through marriage. In marriage the wife's totem is added. When two clans are joined together, such as half fish and half bear, it signifies that the ancestors belonged to the fish and bear clan. Totems are divided into clan, house, individual, burial, historical, and commemorative symbols, and are read from the top down. The idea of the totem is not so unusual when we remember that almost all of the old families of our European ancestors had coats of arms or family crests. Many of these have been handed down and are in use today.

Pictograph Sites

There are several out-of-the-way places in southern Illinois where pictographs and petroglyphs can still be seen. In Gum Spring Hollow, about two miles north of Simpson (Johnson County), there is a painting of Indian origin. Starting from the Illinois Central Railroad at the east end of Gum Spring, it is about three fourths of a mile west up the hollow, on the north side of the creek, to the vertical wall of rock on which the painting is located. This painting has been known to residents of the area for over a hundred years as the "Indian Buffalo Painting." The pictograph, which is about two feet high and four feet long, resembles a buffalo. The Indian who painted it probably used a mixture of red iron-oxide powder and grease that has since faded to a light-rust color.

A group of paintings of Indian origin was reported to be in a rock shelter in Clarida Hollow (Pope County), one of the largest shelters in southern Illinois, by local residents of that area, and investigations substantiated these reports. On the wall in back of this shelter is a group of painted figures and symbols, many of which have weathered so badly that some can no longer be deciphered. These paintings are all red monochromes. Figures which can still be seen are those of a wolf, a turtle, a lizard, and the human form. Other symbols resemble arrows, lines, and outstretched skins of animals. These paintings may have had some religious significance and probably were connected with myth and legend. Other designs, such as the animals, may have been clan or tribal totems which dominated the artistic imagination of these muralists.

Petroglyph Sites

The largest concentration of petroglyphs in southern Illinois has been found in Jackson County. On the west side of Fountain Bluff, north of Grand Tower, facing the Mississippi River, in a rock shelter situated high upon the cliff, there are many petroglyphs. The figures and symbols carved on the wall are the weeping-eye symbol, the equal-arm cross inside of a circle, the swastika inside a circle, human hands and feet, lines, and other unknown characters. At one time there were also several pictographs on the underside of the overhanging roof, but only the figures of a lizard and a human hand painted in red remain.

Peter's Cave, a rock shelter near Kincaid Creek (Jackson County), contained at one time some large rock slabs on which were carved several petroglyphs. Only one, the figure of a bird (thunderbird), remains. Others, one in the form of a bear's head, have been removed.

In Austin Hollow (Jackson County), a half mile north of the intersection of State Highway routes 3 and 151, lying on the west side of the road, is a large sandstone slab known as Turkey Track Rock. This rock gets its name from the number of tracks carved on it resembling "turkey tracks." Many of the designs present are human feet and hands, the weeping eye, the mace, or a ceremonial dagger.

Northeast of Ava, a few miles down the bed of Rock Creek, Jackson County, there is another group of interesting petroglyphs carved in the sandstone outcrop. The designs here consist of human feet and hands, lizards, spiders, snakes, and the human figure.

About seven miles southeast of Vienna (Johnson County), on a hill slope, a number of carvings have been cut into the flat, exposed surface of a sandstone outcrop. The weeping-eye symbol is present along with the cross inside a circle. The most numerous designs present are pairs of human feet placed at different angles over the rock. Several "turkey tracks" are present and, until recent years, a figure depicting a man holding an object in one hand was still visible. Nearby there are several "Indian mortars," holes about ten inches wide and twelve inches deep in a rock, that appear to have been cut out for use as mortars by the Indians.

Recently the author found another group of petroglyphs in a rock shelter, several hundred yards north of the fountain or waterfall on the west side of Fountain Bluff in Jackson County. The petroglyphs in this "art gallery" consist of symbols and figures of birds, animals and the human form. One series of human figures appear to represent a family group; a deer is also represented here and may depict a hunting scene. Many birds are represented and may be thunderbird symbols. Several figures are flying birds or eagles with outstretched talons. There are other figures represented, but they have become so weathered by age that they are no longer decipherable.

Many other petroglyphs and pictographs have been reported in southern Illinois, but have not been investigated. Since this phase of prehistoric Indian art has not been interpreted for southern Illinois, it is possible to give here only locations and descriptions. Interpretation must await further research.

7. Indian Agriculture

Maize: The Indians' Contribution

Our own culture is based on farming and raising livestock; hence, we take these things for granted. They are ways of life which our European ancestors brought with them when they came to live in America. However, the Indians had developed an agricultural way of life before the coming of white men and it is their contribution with which we are concerned. Probably the most important contribution the Indians made to our civilization is agriculture. Many of the crops we grow today were of Indian origin and without these our present economy might be quite different. Maize and also tobacco, tomatoes, potatoes, and many other plants which were cultivated in America were unknown to the rest of the world before Columbus came in 1492.

When the French came to Illinois, they found the "Illinois" Indians engaged in part-time farming. Around their permanent villages the squaws had cornfields, which they cultivated with sharpened hardwood sticks, elk antlers, shoulder bones of elk, and large river-mussel shells. After the crop had been harvested and stored in pits, they would leave the village, often going miles away, and set up temporary camps where they would spend several months in the fall hunting all kinds of animals. This assured them a supply of meat for the remaining cold winter months.

When game was not plentiful there were many kinds of nuts, wild fruits, berries, and many kinds of wild plants with edible leaves, seeds and roots they made use of. Corn, beans and squash were their principal cultivated crops or "staff of life," and they depended on these for a year-around food supply.

Their diet was not as dull as one might suppose; many dishes the Indian women prepared were tasty and delightful. They boiled wild rice; ate the flesh of the bear, elk, deer, bison, beaver, opossum and raccoon; roasted or boiled the "dry" flesh of deer with the fat, juicy flesh of bear, and drank the broth of boiled meats. Squashes were used partly as a substitute for bread and also eaten in summer as vegetables. The crane-neck squash was usually hung up for later use during the winter months.

The labor done by the different sexes was equally divided. To the women fell the duties of rearing children, erecting houses, tending crops, cooking, making baskets and pottery, preparing the skins, and making skin garments for their men and children. The men did the hunting, fishing, trapping, defending the village and making war—a dangerous, serious, exhausting and time-consuming occupation.

In consideration of all the contributions the Indian gave to our culture, especially in agriculture, he most certainly was not on the receiving end of civilization. Among the foods he gave modern man are hominy and corn bread; and nearly half of all the vegetables found in our gardens are of Indian origin.

The ancestors of the Indians not only learned to gather wild plants for their food but, in addition, to plant, cultivate, and develop them. These primitive methods of cultivation through the centuries developed the plants from their wild state to what they are today, and were the beginnings of agriculture in America. Corn alone is one of the greatest contributions of the American Indians to the world. This crop rates among the leading crops now grown, from an economic standpoint. To the Indians of Peru, corn was so important that it became a god. The development of this native American plant by prehistoric Indians has been called the most remarkable achievement in agricultural history. Columbus, on his first voyage to America, found the Indians cultivating this plant. He called it corn, for at that time corn meant all grain in general. Samples of this grain were taken back to Europe and planted as a garden curiosity.

Because Indian corn was the "staff of life," the Indian farmer never took it for granted. Many tribes expressed their gratitude for it in religious rites and tribal ceremonies which accompanied the planting and harvesting of a crop. Because of its importance, the Indians personified corn; Longfellow's "Song of Hiawatha" gives a beautiful account of the legendary origin of Indian corn.

Many Indians honored the Great Spirit for any success they had in farming. A Cherokee legend tells that seven ears of the current crop were to be put aside in order to attract the maize god to the new crop, so that it would have his blessing and grow. When the new crop was ripe, a ceremonial dance took place; only those who had fasted and purified themselves could take part. The seven ears of corn which had been saved from the previous year's harvest were then eaten. In the fall, at harvest time, seven ears were again put aside. In eating the first corn after the dance, care was taken not to blow upon the maize to cool it, for fear of causing a windstorm which might beat down the standing crop in the field.

The English colonists along the Atlantic coast planted both wheat and corn. The wheat they sowed failed but the corn grew. During the first hard winters, corn stood between the colonists and starvation. Corn was the traditional food of the Indian tribes in the historic period and the finding of hidden caches of corn in abandoned Indian villages by our Pilgrim fathers saved the lives of many during severe winters. Their very existence depended on the corn they "borrowed" from the Indians in their absence.

In the early days of settlement, corn became the medium of exchange. The early settlers soon found that they could grow corn in any improvised clearing and a food supply for their families and livestock was assured within a short time. Surplus corn created a growing commerce which encouraged immigration from Europe to the colonies. This assurance of economic as well as personal independence motivated many who sought a better life in the fertile lands of the "Illinois country" early in the nineteenth century.

Scientists have estimated that it required many thousands of years to produce the many corn varieties we grow today; they have so far failed to trace corn's evolution back to wild grasses. A curious plant called pod corn, native to Colombia, South America, has been investigated by those who are tracing the ancestry of corn. One seed-bearing grass has been found which seems to be related to corn grown by the Indians. This grass, native to Guatemala, is teosinte and is of tropical origin.

Many centuries have passed since corn grew in a wild state as grass. Today corn is the most domesticated of all the cereal grains. It must be planted, cultivated, fertilized, and harvested. It was not a self-reproducing crop and was, for centuries, dependent on man's cultivation. Every farm boy knows that such grains as wheat, oats, barley, rye, and other cereal grains can seed themselves but corn cannot. Uncultivated and untended by man, the corn plant would drop its ears at the foot of the stalk and there the kernels would lie. The next year some of the kernels would sprout from the half-buried ear, resulting in a clump of small corn plants so thick that no ears would grow. By the third year the corn would have died out completely. If man should disappear from the earth, corn would be one of the first plants to vanish with him.

White men lived here over four hundred years before they thought of the idea of hybridization of corn. With the development of hybrid corn, in the last two decades, we have been able to produce strains adaptable to almost all soil and climatic conditions in America—places where it would never have grown in its primitive state as Indian corn. Today it is the most efficient plant that we have. Only a small part is consumed directly as corn, but corn products help make modern Americans the best-fed people on earth. Our yearly corn crop now totals around three billion bushels, and has become the basic food plant of our civilization. All of the wealth from corn, the hogs and cattle that feed on it, and the great chemical industries using it, is one of the greatest contributions the Indians have made to our civilization.

Tobacco

As with corn the real story of tobacco begins with the discovery of America. The natives, or Indians, whom Columbus met were using tobacco and offered it to his men as a token of friendship. Botanists believe that tobacco is a native American plant; claims that it grew elsewhere in the world before America was discovered have been rejected by all competent authorities.

Columbus found Indians using tobacco when he first came in contact with them. However, although we are accustomed to thinking that all Indians used tobacco, no trace of it has been found so far in the living places or among the artifacts of some of the early Indian cultures. It was not until much later, probably not until Hopewellian times, that the pipe came into general use in this area. Though the Hopewellians had pipes, it is not known for sure if tobacco was used by them, or a blend of dried herbs. Tobacco may have not been used at this time. The ceremonial use of tobacco was practiced extensively by the Mississippi people —pipes are commonly found among the artifacts of the Hopewellian and the Mississippian cultures—and its use continued on into the ceremonies of the historic Indians.

The history of this herb is closely connected with the legends and folklore of the historic Indians; and its use in rituals was widespread. Among many of the tribes tobacco was held in the greatest veneration, and its raising, gathering, preparation, and blending with other herbs were conducted with great ceremony. In all solemn ceremonies it played an important role; offerings of tobacco were often made to the Great Spirit.

The Indians, from whom our custom of smoking is borrowed, considered the pipe sacred, and places where pipestone was obtained were held in high esteem. A great part of the folklore associated with Indian ceremonials in North America was centered around the calumet, or pipe of peace. This pipe had a great symbolic importance among the historic tribes, and was employed on the most solemn occasions of war councils and peace treaties.

After the discovery of America there was a widespread conviction among Europeans that almost all of the plants of the New World possessed wonderful healing properties. This belief existed partly because Europeans had a great interest in the growth of and trade with the New World. The belief that tobacco had healing power probably was more a European than an Indian idea.

The use of tobaco soon became a habit among white men and it is now used extensively all over the world. From a monetary standpoint, hundreds of millions of dollars are spent each year on the advertising and the selling of this plant, once used by the Indians in their tribal ceremonies and their peace and war councils.

Preservation of Meat

Another practice which the early settlers borrowed from the Indians was a method for preserving meat. Since all Indians depended on the animals they hunted for food, is was necessary to preserve the meat in some way for future use. Soon after an animal was killed, the meat had to be cured. Salt was a scarce item, and it is doubtful if the supply they had was ever sufficient to be used in meat-curing. The only way meat and fish could be preserved was to cure them by drying. The meat was cut up in thin strips and dried in the sun, or hung on a pole-like structure and cured over a slow fire.

Dried meats, cured in this manner, were also pounded and made into cakes called pemmican. These could be stored in dry places in the houses for future use. The Indians, while hunting or on the warpath, carried strips of dried meat to eat. This easy-to-carry, high-protein food was the "K-ration" of the Indian hunter and warrior.

The Use of the Horse

The use of the horse came late in the history of Indian agriculture. The horse was unknown to the American Indians until 1519, when horses were first introduced into America by the Spaniards. At that time Cortez brought the first horses to this country when he landed in Vera Cruz, Mexico. These unknown animals struck terror into the hearts of the Indians, who believed that the man and beast were one animal bent on their destruction. The conquest of Mexico might have been impossible, or at least deferred, had this superstition not caused the Indians to flee before the Spanish conquerors. Later when Coronado began his march into what is now our great Southwest with other horses and other men in his famous search for gold, some of the horses wandered away on their own and others were stolen by the Indians, who by this time found that the Spaniard and his horse were not gods after all.

In Mexico the horse soon became the most important feature of the development of gold and silver mining. Without the horse the transportation of these metals and supplies over mountain and jungle trails would have failed. By the year 1554, large herds of wild horses, descendants of the original sixteen, roamed the country, migrating into what is now New Mexico. At the beginning of the seventeenth century many wild herds were developing throughout the southwest part of the United States.

Apparently the first horses were brought to Illinois from the Southwest, or the Great Plains section of the United States, by the historic Pawnee Indians. They were not, however, the modern-day type of horse, which has been developed over many years from imported European strains. The horse came too late in this area to change the way of living of the Indians as it changed the hunting habits of the plains Indians west of the Mississippi River over a hundred years later. The horse to these western Indians in their wars among themselves was what air power is to a nation today. It increased their range of hunting and raiding many hundreds of miles. In their wars it was always the tribe with the largest number of horses that won.

Horses were very rare among the first French settlers and Indian tribes living in southern Illinois in the early part of the eighteenth century. Oxen were the first animals to be used by the French in clearing land and preparing it for crops. Oxen were brought from France during the settlement of Kaskaskia and Cahokia on the Mississippi River. However, tradition says that the French merchants at Kaskaskia and Cahokia took flatboat loads of furs and produce to New Orleans and purchased horses from the Pawnee Indians, who had brought them from the southwest to this market. The French then sold the flatboats and rode the horses back to southern Illinois.

After the British victory over the French and their Indian allies in the year 1763, horses were imported from Europe. The British at Vincennes, on the Wabash, used trains of pack horses, one tied behind the other, to transport furs over inland trails to this post.

Beginning with the nineteenth century, horses were used as beasts of burden for travel and transportation throughout the Mississippi Valley. The draft horse carried a large part of the burden of transportation and farming throughout the nineteenth and into the first quarter of the twentieth century, but the introduction of mechanical farming has seen the horse gradually disappear from the scene. Today, only show animals and riding horses are left to remind us of an era when the horse was depended upon to furnish the power for most agriculture pursuits. This represents a change in our own culture—a change which men over forty years of age can remember, but which young people of high-school age never saw.

Destruction of the Bison

While the horse is gradually fading from the American scene, the bison vanished completely (except in game preserves) with the settling of the west. When America was discovered, large herds of bison were roaming the entire territory except the Pacific coast west of the Rocky Mountains and a strip along the Atlantic coast.

The American bison, or buffalo, is probably the most imposing animal that ever trod the earth, but many Americans today have never seen a buffalo except on a nickel, where it has been commemorated.

The first reference to these animals by a white man in Illinois was made by La Salle, who sent Father Hennepin on an exploring expedition down the Mississippi River. Hennepin brought back reports and drawings of bison and claimed this animal, which he had seen in large numbers, to be the most interesting of any of the animal life he had encountered on the voyage. Although the bison numbered in the millions at a later time on the western plains, the numbers in Illinois probably never exceeded thousands.

The bison did not last long after the white men came. It survived our hunting methods only a little over a century in Illinois. White men with guns began slaughtering large numbers of them; a French post near Cairo, in southern Illinois, reportedly had collected 13,000 bison hides about the year 1700. Between the hunters and the elements, the fate of the bison in Illinois was sealed, for the terrible winters in central Illinois in the years 1776 and 1778 covered the dead grass with snow for days and many animals starved. Many perished in the blizzards. In the year 1780 remnants of these once numerous herds were seen swimming across the Illinois and Mississippi rivers, heading west. The few that remained soon fell before the guns of the whites. In the year 1810 the bison had almost disappeared from Illinois, and by the year 1820 they were practically extinct east of the Mississippi River.

The bison was a migrating animal; rivers and streams were no barriers to him. Buffalo traces were followed west through Indiana and Kentucky by early white explorers and by the pioneers. These paths were well worn and distinctly visible and often cut into the earth from much use. Early settlers noticed saucer-like depressions, which were beyond a doubt buffalo wallows, on the ground, before the land was plowed.

The bison, like our domesticated animals, was a grazing animal, while deer and elk were more or less browsers, eating twigs and leaves from trees and low shrubs. Unlike most domesticated animals, the bison always faces a storm, because the animal is well-covered with hair in front but has only scanty covering on the rear.

Southern Illinois with its rugged terrain and parklike timber was not a natural habitat for the plains bison. The species of bison living here at the time of the French exploration was the woods bison, a slightly larger animal than the bison of the western plains. The bison was hunted by the Indians, early explorers, and hunters and trappers in the eighteenth century in southern Illinois.

One of the mysteries that have challenged archaeologists excavating village sites of prehistoric southern Illinois Indians is the fact that bones of all the animals hunted by these early Indians have been found in the midden or refuse of their living places except the bones of the bison. Excavators have found buffalo bones in prehistoric Mississippi Indian sites, but their scarcity in sites of older Indian cultures, except in rare instances, raises two possible theories—first, that the bison was here but that Indian hunters only carried the meat home, and not the bones, since they had to depend on the amount each hunter could carry individually; and second, that the bison did not arrive in southern Illinois until about the time the Mississippi culture disappeared, a century before the French explorations late in the seventeenth century.

Part Three

The White Man and the Indian

IN ALL CIVILIZATIONS, primitive or otherwise, people have always been driven by certain incentives or motives which differ from the culture, environment, religion, customs, and traditions of others. Times and conditions always control migration of people. The need for living space and freedom from oppression was the motive for European peoples immigrating to this country. It was the difference in their respective incentives and motives which caused confusion, misunderstandings, and wars between the Indians, French, English, and Americans, whose cultures predominated at different times in southern Illinois.

A. Early French Visitors

1. Marquette

After his trip of exploration down the Illinois and Mississippi rivers, in the year 1673, Marquette made the first observations that give us an insight into the motives behind the struggles of the Indians against the white man in Illinois. Its fine climate, fertile soil, and abundance of all kinds of game caused many a bloody war for its possession, and its famous hunting grounds were known even to the distant Iroquois, who made frequent invasions to drive out the resident tribes.

The Indians prided themselves on their skill as providers from the hunt, and on their bravery in keeping their lands intact. Far too often we think of them as a race of bloodthirsty warriors, entirely overlooking the fact that they welcomed the white men as trusted friends until, bewildered at the strange motives of the white men, they felt themselves losing the land which was rightfully theirs and the game upon which their lives depended.

The Spaniards were first and most active in exploring and

93

settling the New World of North America. Their motive was to duplicate their previous success in finding gold and silver in Mexico and Central and South America. Failing to find gold, they had little effect upon the Indians living in the Illinois country.

2. La Salle

La Salle, the French explorer who had sailed down the Mississippi River in the years 1681-82, recognized the country as a source of revenue and claimed all the trans-Allegheny country, including southern Illinois, for the French. Although the French never purchased any land from the Indians, their few settlers built Cahokia in the year 1699 and Kaskaskia in 1700. These Frenchmen, who came to trap for furs, to trade, and to convert the Indians, lived among the Indians only with the natives' permission. Since their ends were best served by treating the Indians with absolute fairness and with tact, the French adopted the ways and customs of the Indians, encouraging brotherhood and even intermarriage. The bond was so strong between the Indians and French that about the year 1700 the Kaskaskias and several other tribes moved near the new French villages of Kaskaskia and Cahokia. The peace, which endured because of a lack of conflict of ideals, lasted over half a century; however, it came to an abrupt end with the coming of the British after the French and Indian War terminated in a British victory in 1763.

B. The Coming of the British

The British, who had only contempt for the Indians and their customs, wanted to conquer and possess their lands. At first the trusting Indians did not realize that British traders and agents were trading them cheap whiskey, trinkets of little value, and firearms of inferior workmanship. A gun cost an Indian beaverskins stacked to its height—which was probably the reason for the long barrels on some of the traders' guns.

1. The Revolutionary War

When the colonists revolted against British rule, the British surface attitude toward the Indian changed, since the Indian could now help them attain their goal. The Indians could not understand this change of attitude, for now both the English and colonists courted them, offering bounties for scalps. The invasion of the Illinois country by George Rogers Clark, in the years 1778 and 1779, in order to liberate it from the British, caused much confusion among tribes which had been sympathetic to the British. Many, if not most, of the tribes followed their French friends in joining the colonists or in remaining neutral. Shortly after landing at Massac Creek, on the Ohio River, George Rogers Clark and his men captured Kaskaskia on July 4, 1778, and left there on February 6, 1779, overland en route to Vincennes, on the Wabash. His soldiers captured the British garrison on February 25, 1779. The balance of power turned in favor of the colonists and they won all of the Illinois area.

2. Colonial Settlement

After the Revolutionary War there was a flood of colonists into the Illinois country. Some of the colonial soldiers had been paid for their services in the army with land. Other settlers were escaping the social and economic struggles of the older and more crowded eastern part of our young country. During these times when adventurous and hardy settlers were coming into the area, often against the advice of the territorial authorities, a settler by the name of John Lively brought his family to a place on Crooked Creek, now known as Lively Springs, in Washington County. He came here about the year 1811 and in July, 1813, he and his family were killed by a band of Kickapoo Indians, who came from the north to steal horses from the settlers who were living on the "fringe" of the frontier. Communities cling to their pioneer tales and folklore concerning their contacts with the Indians; the author recalls visiting an old man several years ago, in the northwest part of Jackson County, who, knowing of my interest in Indian lore, told me of a white man who reputedly had killed the "last Indian over there in that field." He told me the only reason for the killing was that Lively had seen the Indian out hunting near his cabin and had shot him without provocation. Such stories indicate that both the whites and the Indians were guilty of acts of barbarity.

In pioneer times when the Indians went to war and killed, it was always referred to as a massacre; however, when whole Indian towns were destroyed along with their inhabitants, it was always under the guise of justified military action.

Since the goal of the colonists was to settle new lands and to build permanent homes in this new frontier, it was not long before all the Indians except a few living near Kaskaskia and Cahokia had been pushed northward and westward with the frontier. The struggle between the Indians and white men for dominance, which was ever present during the settling of the frontier country, was caused, in part, by fear and by lack of respect for and understanding of the motives and customs of each other. The two cultures clashed head on. The Indian culture represented a hunting economy based upon unwritten law and tribal government. They utilized the enviroment of land forms, vegetation, water bodies, and animal life as they found it. The American colonists were an agricultural people. They planned to remove the forests, drain the swamps, plow the ground, fence the land, and record ownership for individual use. Their system meant the destruction of the habitat in which the wildlife, the basis of the Indians' economy, lived. Both economies—the hunting, fishing, and gardening of the Indians, and the farming of the colonists—could not occupy the same land or even exist side by side for long. One of the economies or ways of life had to go.

3. Indian Raids

During this period Indian treaties were not honored by the land-grabbing white men. Many Indian tribes were subjected to many inequities of the white conquerors. There were few people during this time who saw the Indian in a friendly and understanding light. They were pushed across the Mississippi River, and it was not many years till the Indian was in his fading glory.

Many injustices were committed on both sides. Many young Indians growing up during these events knew that their very existence was endangered by the motives of the colonists; consequently, they became outlaws, stealing horses from the pioneers and murdering those who ventured beyond the protection of the larger settlements. These raids were, as a rule, not sanctioned by the chiefs or leaders of the Indians, who knew the whites would eventually hold them responsible for these crimes. The following is an example of such an incident:

In July, 1810, a band of Potawatomis from Illinois made a raid on a white settlement in Missouri, killing four people and stealing horses and other property. Early the next year, the territorial governor of Missouri requested that Territorial Governor Edwards of Illinois deliver the Indians responsible for this raid. Captain Levering of Kaskaskia was given a boat, soldiers, and supplies and was commissioned to go to the Potawatomi Indian town near Peoria to make demands for the surrender of the Indians who had participated in the raid. They arrived at Peoria early in August and met the government agent, Forsythe, who had already delivered a message stating Levering's purpose to the principal chief, Massino, better known as Gomo. Gomo was sympathetic toward these demands but had no power to deliver the Indians without the permission of the other chiefs. He made the request that they come to hear the governor's message.

A large number of warriors and chiefs came on August 16, 1810, and after a preliminary talk by Captain Levering and the smoking of the peace pipe, Governor Edwards' address was slowly delivered and interpreted for them. The message told how faithful the President of the United States was to treaty obligations and that his great desire was to have his red and white children live in peace and friendship, with the tomahawk and the scalping knife buried forever. Citing examples of Indian hostility and giving the names of the Indians involved, he went on to say that instant war could be stopped only if the friends and relatives of the white victims were given the Indians responsible for these acts of barbarity to be disposed of as they saw fit. The speech made mention of the British emissaries who had flattered, deceived, and incited the Indians into doing these horrible acts, ending with a full explanation of the power and resources of America.

On the following day Gomo delivered his speech, which was interpreted and copied on the spot.[1] He expressed gladness for

---

[1]Frank E. Stevens, "Illinois in the War of 1812-1814," *Transactions of the Illinois State Historical Society*, Springfield, Illinois, 1904, pp. 89-94.

the opportunity to speak and went on to recount the life of the Indians before the white men came. He followed this account with a summary of the many injustices and inequalities practiced against the Indians by the white men and by an indictment of the white men for their cruelty and greed. Gomo disclaimed knowledge of the deeds of the young Indian warriors who had caused the trouble and indicated that their acts had not been committed with tribal approval.

This story is cited to show that during the conflict between the Indians and white men, many of the atrocities committed by young Indian warriors were not sanctioned by their fellow tribesmen. However, the whole Indian population was blamed for these outrages; and some of the reprisals at the hands of white men claimed many an innocent Indian victim. In our present society we have lawbreakers, but we do not condemn society as a whole. We have set up laws to punish such violators.

4. Indian Resistance to the Colonists

Resistance Under Pontiac

Pontiac became recognized as a great Indian chief when he organized his confederacy to prevent the colonists from gaining possession of the lands stretching from the Alleghenies to the Mississippi River and lying north of the Ohio River that had been ceded to the English by the French in the treaty of 1763. Finally, by carrying out the principles of "divide and conquer," the colonist got the upper hand by making a separate peace treaty with one Indian nation at a time.

Then his great conspiracy failed, the siege of Detroit was lifted, and the Delawares and Shawnees gave in; Pontiac knew he could not save the lands for his tribesmen. He and his families moved farther west. During his life Pontiac married three times, becoming the father of families by his Ojibway wife, his Ottawa squaw, and his Potawatomi spouse.

The Potawatomis settled in northern Illinois and the Ottawas in the vicinity of Starved Rock, near the Illinois River; but Pontiac and his favorite son, Shenebis, came to southern Illinois to live. An unauthenticated legend concerning the tribe which settled near Starved Rock relates that a band of fugitives took refuge on a bluff on the south side of the Illinois River (now La Salle County), where they were besieged by the Potawatomis. Their provisions gave out and the cords of the buckets dropped into the river for water were cut by the enemy. Finally, overcome by hunger and thirst, they were attacked and killed. This beautiful spot is now known as Starved Rock and is one of the state parks of Illinois.

For two years Chief Pontiac lived among the French at Cahokia and across the river in Spanish territory at a trading post now known as St. Louis. Pontiac was now a very disappointed man, forty-nine years of age. Strong drink, which he had striven so hard to keep from his braves, by now had gotten the best of him—he became an alcoholic. He was still troublesome and the French officials at Fort Chartres and the British at Cahokia were still having trouble with his followers. Pontiac could stir up more trouble in a few days than the French could straighten out in months. Too, he always was anxious to renew the fight against the British.

Once he marched with his few remaining braves under the high stone archway of Fort Chartres to see Louis St. Ange, the French commander at the fort, now serving under the British, and said to him: "Father, I have long wished to see you, to recall the battle which we fought together against the misguided Indians and the English dogs. I love the French, and have come here with my warriors to avenge their wrongs."[2] But St. Ange told him the Indians must make peace with the English.

One of the stories related about Pontiac tells that he trusted no one but himself and, because he had been deceived so often by the women of his tribe, he ordered all women from the village when a council of war was being held for fear that information might get into enemy hands. So great was his mistrust that he suspected all and trusted no one. He observed rigorously the rule, "Let not thy left hand know what thy right hand doeth."

Pontiac's last days were spent near Cahokia, where his son Shenebis lived with his family. An English trader, Alexander

---

[2]L. E. Robinson and Irving Moore, *History of Illinois* (New York: American Book Company, 1909), p. 43.

Williamson, fell in love with Shenebis's daughter Elizabeth, the favorite grandchild of Chief Pontiac. Pontiac's hatred for the English was so intense that when he saw his granddaughter associating with an Englishman, he could not control himself. He spent most of his time across the river at St. Louis, but when he did go to Cahokia to visit his son and granddaughter, he was often intoxicated and made open threats against Williamson. Thinking it necessary for his own safety, Williamson hired an Indian belonging to the Peoria tribe to kill Pontiac for a barrel of rum. One evening, after a visit to Cahokia in the year 1769, Pontiac departed over the trail toward St. Louis in an intoxicated condition. He was followed along the trail by the Peoria Indian who hit him in the back of the head with a tomahawk. Pontiac died instantly.

The news spread rapidly among the Indians. Soon the Peoria Indian who had killed Pontiac was found and captured. He was tortured by his Indian captors and forced to reveal the person who was responsible for the crime. When the Indians came with uplifted tomahawks to kill Williamson, it was Pontiac's granddaughter Elizabeth who threw herself between him and his assailants. Indian custom prevented quick revenge, since no Indian dared cross the path of an Indian maiden to take the life of a man when the maiden offered her own life to shield her man from death. They agreed to permit him to live on the conditions that he take Elizabeth for his wife and that he change his name so that no family of Chief Pontiac might have its name tarnished with this crime. Thus, Alexander Williamson became Alexander Williams. After the killing of Pontiac by the Peoria Indian, the Chippewa, the Ottawa, and the Potowatomi Indians fought a tribal war over his death.

So ends the story of a brave chief who, like Tecumseh, made a valiant stand to save the lands of the Indians from the overwhelming pressure of white men in their conquest of the Illinois country. Many Indians are still living who are proud of being descendants of this noted chief.

Resistance Under Tecumseh

Like Pontiac, who had tried earlier to stem the encroachment of the colonists, Tecumseh, the famous Shawnee chief, sought to unite the Indians in a confederation to resist the sale of Indian lands. In July, 1811, Tecumseh brought his witnesses, who were often the women of the tribe, and leaders of the Shawnee Nation to Vincennes to prove the claim of the Shawnees to the lands of southern Illinois.

At the council, William Henry Harrison, governor of the Indiana territory, invited Tecumseh to sit with him on the platform during the conference. The great chief declined and sat on the ground with the other Indians. No agreement was reached and Tecumseh left to organize the Creek, the Choctaw, and the Chickasaw Indians in the south into a league with the tribes of the north.

Historical records tell us that he and an escort of twelve warriors followed the old Indian Trail southward through Bone Gap (now Edwards County) and passed west of the present town of Marion in Williamson County. An early settler by the name of Phelps was surrounded by the Indians south of Marion; Tecumseh talked with him in a friendly manner and inquired about the Massac trail, which he was following south.

In due time, Tecumseh and his braves arrived at their destination. The southern tribes would not join him in his scheme to fight the Americans and, according to tradition, Tecumseh became so infuriated over this that he told these Indians that when he returned to Post Detroit, he would stomp his feet and their houses would fall to the ground. After he had left there on his return home in 1811, the great New Madrid earthquake occurred in December of that year and many of their houses were shaken to the ground.

Tecumseh joined the British in the War of 1812 and was slain at the age of forty-four in the Battle of the Thames in Canada, October 5, 1813. Thus ended the life of one great Indian chief, who, like his predecessor, Pontiac, tried to keep white men from taking lands that rightfully belonged to the Indians.

Pontiac, Blackhawk and Tecumseh were three of the many great Indian personalities who sought justice and honor for their people.

C. Subjugation of the Indians

1. Warfare, Scalping, and Slavery

European nations have fought each other for many hundreds of years.

Indian tribes also fought among themselves, as well as with the white men, although they were not always at war with one another. Although there was more or less fighting in various parts of the region before white men came, the Indians did live at peace with their neighbors for long periods of time. However, in most tribes adult men were considered warriors, and in many tribes their social standing was determined by the number of the enemy they had slain or captured.

In some tribes a state of perpetual feud existed; each tribe, no matter how closely related to another, considered itself an independent nation. Quarreling between these groups resulted in long and bloody feuds. The older men and leaders sometimes talked of peace, yet at the same time extolled the glories of war. Under these conditions peace was almost impossible over a long period of time, and the fear of destruction and sudden death was ever-present.

When a people maintain such ideas, there is only one way for a youth to be respected among his own people and that is the way of the warpath. Even today, in modern nations with strong nationalistic tendencies, the young men are expected to take up military life as a career.

There has been a false impression in America that all Indians were inhuman, and our imagination seems powerless to conceive of or view the Indian in his proper perspective; that is, as trying to hold what was rightfully his and to keep his family life intact. Indians realized that the ways of the white man, with his strange religion and customs, were not always good medicine and were often inconsistent. White men gave the Indians both firewater (whisky) and firearms, a dangerous combination in any society. It is true that during warfare between the white men and the Indians, many atrocities were committed. The Indians sometimes tortured and burned at the stake prisoners whom they had taken captive. But did not white men do the same to those of their own kind whom they accused of witchcraft? The use of poisoned arrows in war has been overemphasized. This overemphasis results from the propaganda used during the historic period. Probably most of us got our ideas about the Indians from the romantic stories of James Fenimore Cooper or from "redskin-bites-the-dust" Westerns.

White men often incited the Indian tribes to war on one another to further their own ends. The Spaniards, the French, the Dutch, the British, and later the American colonists, all claimed parts of America, although these sections were already owned and occupied, and ownership boundaries were recognized by the occupants. The aid of different Indian tribes was eagerly sought by the foreign nations in their wars with each other, and because of the aid which white men gave certain tribes which had traditionally never been at war with one another, they became bitter enemies. Tribal land ownership was thrown into a fluid state and the small Indian nations were picked off one at a time. The French and Indian War was an example of such warfare in which the Indians took sides and fought each other. In their wars the whites as well as the Indians practiced the scorched-earth policy of destruction.

The tragedy of the Indians after the coming of the white men was that they did not understand the rules for competing in our way of life. In one sense they lived somewhat as we do today—in a world full of frustration and conflict. Most of the warfare between the white man and the Indian during the colonial period was caused by white men's trespassing into Indian territory supposedly protected by solemn treaties, which in most cases became nothing more than scraps of paper to be discarded when white men saw that it was to their advantage to do so. We must remember that when America was being settled, the colonists were the aggressors.

In ancient times as well as in the historic period, rivers were most generally tribal boundary lines. Crossing a river meant going to a strange land, among strange people, and could easily mean death to the intruder. Intertribal conflict often resulted when one tribe violated boundaries without permission. This often meant war and sometimes destruction of the weaker tribe. Other times the defeated would flee and seek homes elsewhere.

An example of such forced migration took place about the year 1700, when remnants of the once-powerful Illinois tribes (Kaskaskia and Tamaroa) left their homes on the Illinois River and settled in southern Illinois near the mouth of the Kaskaskia River to escape the dreaded Iroquois.

History, it is interesting to note, does not record any bloody battles in this area between the Indian tribes, with the exception of the one between the Kaskaskias and the Shawnees, in the year 1802, about three miles below the town of old Frankfort. The Kaskaskias were under the leadership of their chief, Jean Baptiste Ducoigne (John Duquoin), then an old man, and a good friend of the whites. The Shawnees were commanded by a chief of rather treacherous nature, which, in all probability, was the cause of the fight. A large number of the Kaskaskias were slain; the remainder fell back on the trail, hotly pursued by the enemy until they reached the Little Muddy River, where, in attempting to cross the swollen stream, the tribe was almost annihilated. The Shawnees after that held undisputed sway until the white settlers steadily and surely drove them across the Mississippi.

While there was more or less fighting between tribes in the early historic period, archaeologists are inclined to think that there was less fighting in prehistoric times, partly because conditions causing tribal war did not exist before white men came. An early period of tranquillity may have existed because there were sufficient resources for all the inhabitants. However, the one thing is certain: Like most nations of today, the inhabitants never arrived at a workable doctrine of a complete Christian brotherhood among all men.

War, a remnant of barbarism, is still with us, only it has risen to gigantic proportions, bringing with it, in our present civilization, spiritual disillusionment and economic distress. In this respect, our civilization is only a stone's throw from the Stone Age. Now, however, the stresses bring on global clashes.

Scalping

While tribal warfare existed before the coming of the white man, contrary to the opinion of many, scalping seems to have started back in the remote ages with the barbarous tribes of the

Eastern Hemisphere, namely among the Scythians and Gauls. In historic times, scalping was practiced exclusively in the north-eastern United States, the point at which many different nation-alities of white men entered.

The New England Puritans, in the year 1673, were the first to offer premiums for native Indian heads and later for scalps. In the year 1724 the colony of Massachusetts offered forty pounds sterling for scalps of women and children. History does not record how they were able to tell the age of the victims. The British government authorized payment of eight dollars for a scalp, and the French and British not only offered premiums for Indians' scalps but also paid for scalps of white enemies. Scalping was completely unknown to the Pueblo and other Indians of the southwest until introduced by the eastern tribes after the coming of the white men. In the wars of extermination between the Indians and the whites on the western plains, Indian scalps some-times brought as much as two hundred to four hundred dollars each. After a time, the success of a war party became based upon the number of scalps it obtained on a raid, and the scalp took on a ceremonial significance, reaching its climax on the western plains in the scalp dance.

Slavery

No one knows when slavery was first practiced in Illinois. When Father Marquette, the French explorer, came to the Illinois country in the year 1673, he found slavery in existence among the Illinois Indian tribes. Just how far this age-old custom extends back into prehistoric Indian times is not known, but it is generally supposed that it had been practiced for hundreds and probably thousands of years.

It is known, however, that in the wars among themselves, the historic Indian tribes generally spared the lives of the women and children they captured. Sometimes, when the women and young children would be traveling or gathering food, they were captured by a unfriendly tribe and held captive for long periods of time. The women and children were taken into the tribe and assigned to different members of the tribe. Older women were put to work doing much of the heavy work around the village, such as gardening and food-gathering. Younger women were sometimes chosen as wives by men in the tribe, thereby becoming members of the clan.

All nationalities who have lived in southern Illinois have had slaves. The French, who were the first to import Negro slaves into this area as early as the year 1719, used them for farming and other labor. The Cherokees, who passed through southern Illinois on their forced migration to the Indian territory in the years 1838-39, had Negro slaves, which suggests that this custom was widespread among the Indians as well as among the white men during the historic period of our country and up to the close of the Civil War in 1865.

2. Forced Migration and Subjugation

After the French period in southern Illinois, there was little effort made to assimilate the Indians by intermarriage. Some people in southern Illinois today point with pride to the fact that some Indian blood flows in their veins, but one hundred years ago it was considered a disgrace. This refusal of the white men to accept the Indians as human individuals and to intermarry with them, in addition to the difference in land use, meant that the Indians must be killed or forced to migrate. Although some white men, including leaders in the pioneer society, felt and knew that the Indians were mistreated, the pressure among the whites was so great that the leaders shut their lips and eyes and salved their consciences by agreeing to move the Indians to "good lands" out west. The Indians could go west and live on lands that white men did not yet want and which were already owned by other Indians.

Soon after the War of 1812 the last Indians were forced from their lands in Illinois. The Blackhawk War ended in 1832, and after this last struggle of the Indians to keep their land, they were compelled to leave Illinois. The Kasakaskia Indians, a remnant of a once-powerful Illinois tribe who for over a century had lived near the mouth of the Kaskaskia River, were moved west by the United States government about the year 1833, ending forever the Indians' rights to lands in southern Illinois.

While moving to reservations in the west, many Indian tribes crossed Illinois. The Cherokee trek, one of the largest and most famous, passed through southern Illinois under military escort in the fall and winter of 1838-39. This forced exodus of the Chero-kees is a good example of the general hatred toward the Indians during the nineteenth century.

The Cherokees were civilized Indians; perhaps more civilized than their white pioneer neighbors. They had a great teacher Sequoyah, who created for his people an alphabet by which every Cherokee could learn to read his own language. Many were devout Christians and among them were many ministers of the gospel, teachers, and intelligent leaders.

Andrew Jackson and his successor Martin Van Buren disliked Indians. President Van Buren argued that no state could achieve proper culture, civilization, and progress as long as Indians were permitted to remain within its boundaries.

In the year 1838, the military began to round up all the Cherokees and placed them in stockades to be sent away from their ancestral home in the Great Smoky Mountains to the Indian territory set aside for them across the Mississippi River. They were brought in from the mountains of North Carolina and Tennessee, and from Georgia, and from Alabama, which was the great stronghold of the Cherokee Nation.

This was to be the beginning of the most infamous "death march" in American history. None were spared; the young and the very old were forced to take the cold, weary trail westward to a new homeland in the wilderness of the Arkansas and Oklahoma territory. Only a few escaped in the vastness of the Smoky Moun-tains. They remained so well hidden in the forests that no white soldiers could find them. The descendants are now living peaceful, useful lives in and around Cherokee, North Carolina.

After leaving their homeland they passed through Nashville, Tennessee, and northward through Hopkinsville, Kentucky, and were ferried across the Ohio River into southern Illinois at Golconda. This great cavalcade consisting of wagons, carriages, horsemen and plodding people was so large that there never seemed to be an end to it, so many thousands were always coming.

The people in southern Illinois were not hospitable or kind to the refugees, who often met with unkindness and cruelty. Some-times they were not permitted to pitch their tents or cut fire wood along the way. When they finally arrived in Union County, where the ridges rise high from the Mississippi flood plain, they found the Mississippi River full of massive ice floes. They could not cross. It was wintertime and that year found the season to be severely cold for southern Illinois. Spread out on the trail in small camp groups, eight thousand Cherokees camped for two weeks east and west of Jonesboro, waiting for the ice-filled river to clear so they could cross. In those two weeks of terrible, frigid winter weather, many died—for them it was the end of the trail. Nearly two thousand of the thirteen thousand Cherokees died before they reached the Oklahoma Territory.

It was at one of the Cherokee camps on Dutch Creek, west of Jonesboro, that Basil Silkwood purchased the quadroon girl Priscilla from a Cherokee chieftain. He took her to his home near Mulkeytown, east of Duquoin. Here she lived a free woman with the Silkwood family the remainder of her life.

The town of Wetaug in Pulaski County gets its name from a Cherokee chief who died here during that winter in southern Illinois.

Many who travel over Highway 146, between Golconda and Ware, Illinois, scarcely give it a thought that a little over a century ago, one of the greatest tragedies ever to befall a civilized Indian nation took place along this highway. The stories of the distress they suffered from cold, hunger and disease would fill a book. This "death march" has been memorialized by historians as the "trail of tears." For many of these displaced people, the trail of tears ended for them in southern Illinois.

This practice of forced migration was in strong contrast to the condition of the Indians in Mexico, where the Spanish intermarried with the Indians, and in parts of Canada, where the French and Indians intermarried. In both of these areas assimilation was far more widespread. One may well question why Indian reservations in the United States are still in existence, particularly in view of the fact that, contrary to public opinion, all Indians now living in the United States are not wards of the government.

It was only a century and a half after the first French explorers came that the Indians were expelled from Illinois and forced to give up their way of life and accept the ways of the white man. There are still echoes of the red man. Archaeologists are continuing to unearth and interpret these echoes.

Do not these echoes serve to remind us that it is difficult for a culture to give up its way of life? Is one culture not loath to have its way of life changed entirely or dominated by another?

In the complex mechanical age of the twentieth century do not the echoes of the red man make us mindful of the simple life he lived, of his industry and his art, of his constant struggle for existence against the forces of nature and against the power of the white man, and his contribution to our own culture?

If we listen long enough to these echoes of the red man, is it not possible that we may ask ourselves, "Is there not a real kinship between the historic red man and the white man of the twentieth century?"

Were not many of the red man's problems twentieth-century problems? Are we not confronted with the problem of combating the forces of nature and the forces of would-be conquerors? Are we not confronted, as the red man was, with the problem of living peaceably with our fellow men?

The Piasa Bird

THE FIRST REFERENCE by a white man to an Indian painting on the limestone bluffs overlooking the Mississippi River was made by Father Marquette, the French explorer on his voyage down this river in the year 1673.

This painting of the Piasa[1] (man-eater) has a strong local tradition to this day. Although the original disappeared many years ago, several replicas have been repainted in its place by white men to commemorate and keep alive this old Indian tradition.

The story of the killing of this great bird by Ouatoga (Wa-to-ga), Chief of the Illini, and his one hundred expert bowmen has been handed down by the Indians.

Each morning, the strill screams of the Piasa Bird as it flew down the river brought fear to the minds of the Illini and chilled the blood of the Indian youth. Dozens of Indian boys and girls had been carried away in the talons of the Piasa Bird to be devoured in its great cave near what is now Grafton, Illinois.

Ouatoga was getting old and his chief concern was the destruction of this terrible killer. He called his braves into council on the hills nearby and told them he was going to pray to the Great Spirit who would tell him what to do.

Chief Ouatoga went into the hills and on the highest bluff he communed with the Great Spirit. He prayed that some plan for the destruction of this Piasa Bird be given him. The Great Spirit answered and told the Chief, "Dip your arrows deep and well into the poison of the copperhead snake and fire them into the body of the Piasa Bird; they will cause its death."

---

[1]Pronounced Pi-a-saw.

111

Ouatoga returned to the Illini camp. He told the braves what the Great Spirit had communicated to him. The plan was for someone to risk his life by standing on the edge of the cliff at the break of day. When the Piasa Bird swooped down to sink his talons into the victim, one hundred poisoned arrows would be loosed by strong bowmen and sent through the scaly crust of the Piasa Bird.

All of the braves begged to take the place on the cliff, but the old Chief said, "I am old and I will make the sacrifice."

The Indians went out in the hills to catch copperhead snakes that they might draw their poison and have plenty in which to dip their arrows. Finally, all was arranged. The one hundred arrows had been dipped into the poison and all the braves had practiced bringing their bowstrings back to the lobes of their ears. This was the strength needed to pierce a thick hide, tough as that of a buffalo.

Ouatoga communed with the Great Spirit all night. "Great Spirit, think not of my life, but think of the sons and daughters of the Illini."

All was arranged. Every brave was shown his place in the woods overlooking the cliff. He said to his braves, "Fear not. The Great Spirit will direct your poisoned arrows, but aim carefully."

At last, the first pink gleam of daylight came in the East and Ouatoga pulled his red blanket about him and raised his head to commune with the Great Spirit. Sound could be heard, the scream of the Piasa Bird. It was hungry and was seeking its breakfast. Down the center of the Mississippi River it flew, looking for victims on the banks. As the bird neared the cliff where the old Chief stood, it let out a terrific scream and flew straight towards him, circling and circling above its victim to make sure all was well. Finally, the great bird set its wings and started down to pick up the Indian in the red blanket. Chief Ouatoga did not move. He felt that the Great Spirit was there with him; as he clutched with all his strength the sturdy roots which grew there.

With a mighty scream the Piasa Bird swooped down and grabbed its victim when the one hundred braves rose up and one hundred poisoned arrows were loosed with such speed as the occasion demanded. Every arrow hit its mark and the Piasa Bird dropped with a great scream of terror into the Mississippi River and sank beneath its murky surface.

The warriors very tenderly carried the bleeding mangled form of old Chief Ouatoga down the bluff to his lodge. The medicine man placed his ear over the old man's heart and found that it was beating weakly. They gave him loving care, and one morning they were rewarded by seeing the old man open his eyes to find himself safe with his people.

There was great rejoicing in the tribe. A large feast was planned. The hunters brought fowl, fish, and fresh meat from the hunt. The braves decked themselves in their finest belts of wampum and their finest feathers. The women put on their beaded garments. The feast was held that night around the fire which had burned since noon when the sun was high. Far into the night they ate and drank, danced and beat their tomtoms.

The next morning, old Terahionanaka (Tera-hi-on-a-na-ka), the arrow maker, carefully mixed his paints and carried them to the top of the great bluff and there, in flaming colors, painted the picture of the Piasa Bird.

Thereafter, every time Indians went down the river they each fired an arrow at the picture on the bluff in memory of their deliverance from the terrible Piasa Bird.

Selected Bibliography

Books

Belting, Natalia Maree: *Kaskaskia Under the French Regime.* Urbana, Illinois, University of Illinois Press, 1948.

Cole, Fay-Cooper: *Kincaid, A Prehistoric Illinois Metropolis.* Chicago, The University of Chicago Press, 1951.

Cole, Fay-Cooper, and Deuel, Thorne: *Rediscovering Illinois.* Chicago, The University of Chicago Press, 1937.

Cole, Mabel Cook, and Cole, Fay-Cooper: *The Story of Primitive Man.* Chicago, University of Knowledge, Inc., 1940.

Collier, John: *Indians of the Americas.* New York, The New American Library, 1947.

Conant, A. J.: *Foot-prints of Vanished Races.* St. Louis, Chancy R. Barnes, 1879.

Cushman, H. B.: *History of the Choctaw, Chickasaw, and Natchez Indians.* Greenville, Texas, 1899.

Deuel, Thorne: Hopewellian Communities in Illinois. *Scientific Papers,* Vol. V, Springfield, Illinois, State Museum, 1952.

Garretson, Martin S.: *The American Bison.* New York, Zoological Society, 1938.

Griffin, James B.: *Archaeology of Eastern United States.* Chicago, The University of Chicago Press, 1952.

Haggard, Howard W. (M.D.) : *Devils, Drugs, and Doctors.* New York, Pocket Books, Inc., 1946.

Houck, Louis: *History of Missouri,* 4 vols. Chicago, 1908.

Keithahn, Edward L.: *Monuments in Cedar.* Ketchikan, Alaska, Roy Anderson Company, 1945.

Knoblock, Byron W.: *Banner Stones of the North American Indian.* LaGrange, Illinois, Published by author, 1939.

Lilly, Eli: *Prehistoric Antiquities of Indians.* Indianapolis, Indiana, Indiana Historical Society, 1937.

Longfellow, Henry W.: *The Poetical Works of Longfellow.* Boston,

James Rosgood and Company, 1875.

MacGowan, Kenneth: *Early Man in the New World*. New York, The Macmillan Company, 1950.

Martin, Paul S., Quimby, George I., and Collier, Donald: *Indians Before Columbus*. Chicago, The University of Chicago Press, 1947.

Maxwell, Moreau S.: *Woodland Cultures of Southern Illinois*. Beloit, Wisconsin, Beloit College, 1951.

McAdams, William: *Record of Ancient Races in the Mississippi Valley*. St. Louis, Missouri, C. R. Barns Publishing Co.

Nida, William Lewis: *The Story of Illinois and Its People*. Chicago, O. P. Barnes, 1910.

Parkman, Francis: *La Salle and the Discovery of the Great West*. Boston, Little, Brown and Co., 1931.

Robinson, L. E. (A.M.), and Moore, Irving: *History of Illinois*. New York, American Book Company, 1909.

Stevens, Frank E.: Illinois in the War of 1812-14. *Transactions of the Illinois State Historical Society*, Springfield, Illinois, Phillips Brothers State Printers, 1904.

Waller, Elbert: *Waller's History of Illinois*. Galesburg, Illinois, Wagoner Printing Company, 1929.

Wissler, Clark: *Indians of the United States*. Garden City, New York, Doubleday and Company, Inc., 1949.

Archaeological Journals

Fowler, Melvin L: The Ethel R. Wilson Site: A preliminary report. *Journal of the Illinois State Archaeological Society*, *I*:3:January 1951.

Goddard, Pliny, Early: Indians of the Northwest Coast. *The American Museum of Natural History Handbook*, Series No. 10. New York, American Museum Press, 1934.

Hall, E. N.: Prehistory of Hardin County. *History of Hardin County, Illinois*. Written by the Historical Committee for the Centennial, 1931.

Logan, Wilfred D.: Graham Cave, an archaic site. *Memoir of the Missouri Archaeological Society*, *2*, Columbia, Missouri, Missouri Archaeological Society, 1952.

Maxwell, Moreau S.: The succession of woodland and horizons in the Carbondale area. *Illinois Academy of Science Transactions*, *40*, 1947.

Neumann, Georg K.: The Hopewellian Culture in the Lower Wabash

Valley. *Journal of the Illinois State Archaeological Society*, *I*:4: April 1951.

Peithmann, Irvin: Certain bluff shelters on Indian Creek in Jackson County, Illinois. *Bulletin of the Illinois State Archaeological Society*, *I*:1:1938.

———: Evidences of early woodland culture at Chalk Bluff Rock Shelter. Reprinted from *American Antiquity Journal*, *IV*:3:January 1939.

———. Pictographs and petroglyphs in Southern Illinois. *Journal of the Illinois State Archaeological Society*, *II*:4:April 1952.

———: Recent Hopewell finds in Southern Illinois. *Journal of the Illinois State Archaeological Society*, *V*:2:October 1947.

———: The archaeology of Southern Illinois. *Illinois State Archaeological Society*, Parts I and II, April, July 1951.

———: A preliminary report on salt making and pottery manufacture at a prehistoric site in Gallatin County, Illinois. *Journal of the Illinois State Archaeological Society*, *III*:3:September 1953.

———: A preliminary report on excavations at the Jones Site, Williamson County, Illinois. *Journal of the Illinois State Archaeological Society*, *II*:2 and 3:October 1951, January 1952.

Stephens, B. W.: Engraved shell gorgets from Illinois. *Transactions of the Illinois State Academy of Science*, *32*:2:May 1939.

Thomas, Cyrus: Alexander County, Illinois, Indian diggings. *12th Annual Report of the Bureau of Ethnology, 1890-1891*, Government Printing Office, Washington, D. C., 1894.

Thomas, Joe C.: Dust, bones and rocks. *Journal of the Illinois State Archaeological Society*, *VI*:2:October 1948.

Thompson, Scerial: The Cherokee Cross Egypt, *Journal of the Illinois State Historical Society*, Winter 1951.

Periodicals

Deevey, Edward S., Jr.: Living records of the Ice Age. *Scientific American*, May 1949.

Ford, James A.: Mound builders of the Mississippi. *Scientific American*, March 1952, pp. 23-27.

Gastiglioni, Arturo: The use of tobacco among the American Indians. *Ciba Symposia*, *4*:11 and 12, February-March 1943.

Roberts, Frank H. H.: The early Americans. *Scientific American*, *184*:2:1951.

Solecki, Ralph: How man came to North America. *Scientific American*, *184*:2:January 1951.

Bulletins

Beilmann, August P., and Brenner, Louis G.: The changing forest flora of the Ozarks. *Annals of the Missouri Botanical Garden, 38*: 261-282, September 1951.

————: The recent intrusion of forest in the Ozarks. *Annals of the Missouri Botanical Garden, 38*:261-282, September 1951.

Branegan, James A.: Chemistry and science in prehistoric America. *National Archaeological News, I*:9:November 1939.

Bryan, Kirk: Flint quarries—the sources of tools and, at the same time, the factories of the American Indian. *Papers of the Peabody Museum of American Archaeology and Ethnology, XVII*:3: Cambridge, Massachusetts, Harvard University Museum, 1950.

Cahokia Brought to Life. Published by the Greater St. Louis Archaeological Society. St. Louis, Wellington Printing Co., 1950.

Deuel, Thorne: Illinois records of A. D. 1000. *Journal of the Illinois State Historical Society, XLI*:3:219-230, September 1948.

————: *Man's Venture in Culture.* Story of Illinois, No. 6. Springfield, Illinois, Illinois State Museum, 1950.

Eifert, Virginia S.: *Illinois Mammals, Today and Yesterday.* Story of Illinois, No. 2. Springfield, Illinois, Illinois State Museum, 1951.

Hornaday, William T.: The Extermination of the American Bison. *Annual Report of the Board of Regents of the Smithsonian Institution,* Part II. Washington, Government Printing Office, 1889.

Moyer, W. N.: The Seven Wonders of Egypt. *Journal of the Illinois State Historical Society, XXVII*, 1934.

Index